AT SEA: AWAITING ORDERS

FR. COLUM KELLY

Edited by
JOSIE EDWARDS

Illustrated by
BRYONY WATSON

This book is dedicated to the memory of

Frank and Gretta.

When Bennett Street met Sloan's Terrace

FOREWORD
BY ROSE GEORGE

What I remember most is the lunch. There wasn't any. Over the years it became a joke between us: that Colum Kelly operated on so much energy, he didn't need sustenance, and he forgot that lesser mortals did. I start with that deprecating anecdote not to diminish Colum but the opposite: in fact Colum forgot about lunch because he was sustained on his own formidable energy, not because he was unkind to his hungry guest. Anyone who meets Colum soon learns that kindness and he go together like salt and seawater.

I didn't really know what to expect when I arrived at Immingham. I'd barely heard of the place, though I lived under 50 miles away, and though I had been researching my book on shipping for a while. The view as I drove to the port was forbidding: chemical towers, warehouses, not many humans. The security was equally intimidating, with gate-houses and ID checks. I thought I was coming to a port, not a prison. But ports these days must be secure and locked-off, which is partly why the general public is so ignorant of the lives of people who work on those ships that they may see offshore from a beach and think nothing of. They see the ship, but not the men bringing their breakfast cereal, their milk bottles, their sugar, through winter storms.

Colum Kelly, by contrast, thinks everything of these men and the occasional woman. When I met him, he was so connected with the port, the ships were practically in his living room, so close did they pass to his window, in his small flat above the seafarers' centre. It had the feel of a flat that was shelter and not much more, because when did Colum find the time to be in it? He was always in motion somewhere, up and down gangways, driving to Argos, milling around in the seafarers' centre chatting to the Filipino, Ukrainian, Chinese, Polish seafarers who had come to Skype, to drink a beer, to be somewhere that wasn't the ship they had been on for months, to talk to someone who wasn't their shipmate. They could not do better than to talk to this Irish priest who travelled from an inner-city Leeds parish to this unlikely one, and never wanted to leave. Sometimes, Colum's work is clearly vital, because seafarers in trouble on their ships – where they can often be abused or have wages withheld -- often find the ear of a priest a much safer outlet than any official helpline. Sometimes Colum's work seems derisory or trivial. Perhaps it is simply a matter of sourcing some new batteries or hair gel. But new batteries after weeks of not having batteries matter. Hair gel on a ship with no toiletries left matters. A smile, a visit, a mass in the mess room over lunch plates: when you have been at sea for months and missed your family's birthdays and sometimes births and deaths, all this matters. In my book I called Colum's work "the ministry of small gestures," but just because the gestures are small doesn't mean that the impact of Colum's work has not been huge. I know that around the world there are thousands of seafarers who will remember this prosaic northern English port, not for the scenery of coal heaps and industrial zones, but for the Irish priest who climbed up their gangway, who waited for an invitation into their living quarters, who, as soon as he could, would ask his most important question: "How can I help you?"

I bet they counted themselves lucky to meet Colum, and so do I.

Rose George is a British journalist and author of *Ninety Percent of Everything* (about shipping).

For more information on her newest release, *Nine Pints*, see https://www.rosegeorge.com

INTRODUCTION

The handshake was firm and the smile on the cook's face told me he was pleased I had visited the ship. But something felt different. A small piece of paper was clasped between our hands. I discreetly screwed it up, stuffing it in my pocket to read when I was clear of the ship.

Unfolded, it read: *No salary 9 months. Please help.*

This is ministry in the raw.

"Immingham? Where's that then?"

I have to admit the name Immingham was a mystery to me too when I was appointed Port Chaplain sixteen years ago. This vast and mighty port covers a huge swath of the South bank of the Humber estuary, with Grimsby just down the road and Hull across the river. But it became home to me, and the place where I have found most challenges and fulfilment in my ministry.

I lived in a small flat above the Seaman's Mission, the only person who had an address on Immingham Dock. This is how close the ships came to my kitchen window.

From my lofty position I could look right across the port every morning, checking who had come into the parish during the night and who had left; God bless them and keep them safe on their travels.

Originally it was planned that I would only be there for about three months, but the excitement of working in outreach to the stranger captivated me. Sixteen years later, I was still there and as enthusiastic as ever about this wonderful work of the Church.

Over forty-six years as a priest, and indeed, in the years as a member of the laity before that, I have felt privileged to be a part of that mission. I have been excited and sometimes surprised by the variety of all I have been asked to do.

I have served for thirty years in traditional parish ministry, working in many chaplaincy situations, schools, hospitals, prisons. However, in my work with the Apostleship of the Sea, now called Stella Maris, I found new and dynamic ways to serve the Lord in the call to mission to the people of the sea. I am so proud to share the vision of Stella Maris, participating in the Church's mission of outreach.

Sixteen years on, the old knees aren't as keen as they were and the sight of a hundred steps on a gangway is a challenge too far. Luckily there are two new young and fit chaplains whose knees don't buckle at the prospect; Steve and Bryony, fit, active and enthusiastic. They are the new faces of Stella Maris and their commitment and devotion to the welfare of seafarers guarantees that the mission is in good hands.

My role now is to pass on my experience and enthusiasm to other chaplains around the world, and to help them understand the great privilege of making a difference to the seafarers they encounter.

Hopefully in the pages ahead you will get some understanding of the work involved and some insight into the lives of the people of the sea for whom we care.

1

IMMINGHAM

A word about Immingham.

Have you ever been to a working cargo port? I think maybe not, few have.

The vast expanse of the port is hard to envisage, even for those who make visits and see a small area of the dock. Perhaps you have been on a ferry crossing or cruise, but there you see nothing of the reality of a working port.

It's not surprising, for ports are mysterious places, a touch of the invisible about them.

Here's a thought.

Can you remember getting up this morning and the time spent before rushing out your front door? Think of all the things involved in your routine: your alarm clock or phone. The bedding, the bed itself. The clothes and shoes you put on. Your kettle, the fridge, toaster—maybe you watched the morning news or listened to the radio; even checked your emails.

We take for granted most of the things we need to make our morning routine happen, but they have been brought by sea, and the lives of the people who brought them remains a mystery. Add to the list as you need, and hopefully it will help you understand how dependent we are on seafarers and the ships they man.

Let me give you an example.

One afternoon a captain asked me to help him buy a tablet. I took him to the nearest PC World and while he was looking at the various options, the store manager came along, smiling and doing his 'customer-friendly' bit.

I told him that the Captain was a seafarer. He smiled but obviously needed to move on to the next customer.

"Do you know how important seafarers are to your store?" I asked. I set him a challenge as we looked around the store with its vast banks of televisions, fridges, freezers, phones, Hi-Fi units, washing machines and dryers. "Find me one thing in this store that hasn't arrived by sea."

Just as we were leaving, he came to me. "I get your point, but what about this?" He held up a small paper till roll. "This hasn't come by sea. You can see; it says 'Made in UK'."

"It has," I said. "The paper to make that has come by ship from Scandinavia."

Here in Immingham we see such a wide variety of cargo coming into the port that the message is pretty obvious. We see such things as building materials, crude oil imported here to be refined into fuel for our transport, coal imported from South America, China, South Africa, even Australia.

Chemicals and gas tankers bring their fuels. Biomass comes from Canada. Vast containers are filled with white goods, clothes and IT equipment. Steel, iron ore, and biomass pass through. Car-carrying ships bring thousands of new vehicles every day.

One million tonnes of coal arrive in Immingham every month, mainly to keep our power stations fired up. This in turn keeps the electricity flowing through the network to keep our gadgets working and our homes heated.

However, coal imports are gradually diminishing, as there is more emphasis now on renewable sources of energy. The sight of huge wind turbines at sea may not fill everyone's soul with joy, but they are becoming a more common feature of our shoreline. We are seeing a different landscape in the port. Where once there seemed to be mountains of coal everywhere, we now see acres of land covered in vast swathes of turbine fins.

This all sounds incredibly industrial, and it is; there's no two ways about that. But all the same, Immingham Port has a rare beauty all of its own. It is difficult to explain this to folk who have never seen it and maybe even more difficult to enthuse about the beauty of the place to those who do visit.

When I arrived here, I was struck by the enormity of everything. The sheer bulk of the ships in their various colours and flags, the heavy machinery on the roads that transport cargo from one site to another. The constant noise, the clinkity-clank of chains, and the long arms of cranes going about their business with the precision and grace of a ballet dancer in pre-pirouette glissade. In its own way, all that is beautiful.

2

A DAY IN THE LIFE

The work we do in Stella Maris is never dull because it is always so varied. Let me give you an example just of the events of one day...

When I got my newspaper that morning, the headlines were accompanied by a picture of coal terminal stevedores holding placards proclaiming '100 Million Tons of Coal' (in nine years). In a year when the port celebrated its centenary, yet another milestone had been passed.

What the story couldn't tell was that earlier in the day the Border Agency had removed cocaine with a street value of several million pounds from one of the ships in port. The cargo had been loaded in Columbia, and inspected by customs in Rotterdam, where there had been a partial discharge of the cargo. It then went on to Immingham where intelligence had been received that the cocaine was on board, and subsequently the drugs were found.

There was no suggestion that the crew had any part in this but while the long search went on, the men were confined to the ship and visitors were turned away. Situations like this cause great anxiety for the crew. It is important to remember a ship is not just a huge piece of metal that carries vast amounts of cargo around the world; it is their home for the length of the contract.

Anyone walking on a quayside seeing these mighty beasts will perhaps find it difficult to imagine these really are people's homes. All chaplains understand this and when they climb aboard, they know that they are on someone's doorstep and must await an invitation to enter the living quarters.

Imagine how you would feel if a large group of people invaded your privacy poking into every nook and cranny of your home. That's how the crew felt. They were also anxious that the search would delay the discharge and the ship might miss its departure slot and the arrival slot at their next port.

I was allowed on the ship to bring phone cards to the crew, who were anxious that they had not been able to call home to reassure family that they had arrived safely at their next destination. The men understood that these things happen but were very low in spirits at their 'captivity'. Once the drugs had been taken away, the crew came to the Centre where they were able to make contact with their families.

Later in the day, the agent of a small ship called to see if I could help with a captain arrested for being over the legal limit prior to the ship leaving port. By the time I got to the ship, the Captain had already been taken away by the police. The reading on the breathalyser had been 154; the legal limit is 35.

It all got a bit farcical after that: the Chief Mate took a call from the owner, inquiring if he was able to sail the ship to Belgium. He agreed to and when I enquired about his Master's ticket, he said he had it somewhere but wasn't sure where. He said he felt he should be able to sail the ship but was unsure about the computers on the bridge.

If the ship was to sail, the Captain's kit needed to be taken off. I visited him in the cells in Grimsby to see what he needed.

The Duty Sergeant took me to one side. "There's been a development. Although he registered 154 with our mobile kit, the station machine shows 39. Normally if it's under 40 we let them go, but I'm not sure if there is a different ruling in the maritime world." Cue a call to Maritime Coastguard Agency experts who then visited the ship.

I brought the angry Master back to his ship and endured a long rant about the British. He sailed out around midnight.

That evening an Indian crew was brought in by our driver. The cook came over to me and said, "Six months ago you visited our ship to celebrate Mass but were unable to stay for dinner; so tonight we bring dinner to you." He gave me a box of beautifully spiced chicken, some vegetable dhal and three chapattis.

All in a day's work—what a wonderfully varied world we inhabit!

But the variety doesn't stop there.

Chaplains often work in a lonely world isolated from colleagues for much of the time. But in many countries a covenant exists between the major Churches that encourages us to work interdenominationally. So for example in major ports there may be a chaplaincy team from Stella Maris, Mission to Seafarers, Fisherman's Deep Sea Mission and Sailor's Society.

In my final days in Immingham I was fortunate to work alongside two colleagues: David from the Sailor's Society and Cameron from the Mission to Seafarers. They were both very experienced in the maritime world. Cameron had served for many years as a Chaplain in Jordan and David, a Methodist minister, had a long history of service as a communication officer in the Merchant Navy.

I loved the stories David told of his time as Radio Officer: while on distant shores he forwarded the men's pool slips to Littlewoods by Morse code. He was able to tap out orders for special occasion cards and gifts to arrive at family homes.

Ah, those were the days….

We came from very different Church backgrounds but respected each other's traditions and gave great encouragement to one another. We worked with the guiding principle that we would:

• Provide religious ministry and support to those of our own faith.

• Facilitate for all religious beliefs, and none.

• Support all seafarers and their families.

In general we met together, prayed together, visited ships and if there were any issues on board that would be specific to one chaplain, the information was passed on. For example if there was a request from a crew seeking Mass on the ship, I would be contacted by the visiting chaplain.

I enjoyed working with all the chaplains I have encountered. Each year I delight in the invitation to Markfield Institute of Higher Education where I speak to Muslim chaplains just prior to the completion of their studies.

The need is growing for Muslim chaplains in Further and Higher Education, the National Health Service (including hospices), social welfare, prisons, the Police, Armed Forces and Industry. There's no mention in that list of seafaring chaplaincy, so why do they invite me?

The students are interested in the diversity of the mission we carry to people of all denominations. Of course they are fascinated by the stories I bring, but keen also to learn about the things we share in common the very nature of our chaplaincy. Most of the students will find placements in NHS or prison environments where they too "go to where people are hurting".

Last year I was able to reflect with them on the covenant signed by Pope Francis and Sheikh Ahmed al-Tayeb, the head of Sunni Islam's most prestigious seat of learning. The document pledges that al-Azhar and the Vatican will work together to fight extremism, in the name of "all victims of wars, persecution and injustice." Learning together adds such richness to the work.

3

STELLA MARIS

I became associated with this great ministry in 2004. I had read much about how this charity was developing and felt a call to join in some way in this great apostolate. Until then my work had been parish-based, serving communities across West Yorkshire, with a large amount of chaplaincy involved mainly in hospitals and schools.

I talked it over with my Bishop. It was agreed I could spend a year with the Apostleship of the Sea, and the position would be reviewed after that. I met with Commodore Chris York, then National Director, who suggested I become port chaplain for the south bank of the Humber, based on Immingham dock. At that time I was the only priest serving full time in UK ports.

I took up residence in the small bedsit above the Seafarer Centre, right on the edge of the lock, and that was my home for sixteen happy, fulfilling years. Although very different from ministry as I had known it, there were some striking similarities that made the transition feel quite natural.

Two phrases in the handbook 'Duties of Chaplains' appealed greatly:

Be alongside

with its maritime terminology invites you to to stand by the seafarer in the harsh, cruel and often unjust world they inhabit. Let them be confident of your loyalty in a world where they may not have many advocates.

Welcome the stranger

is a basic tenet of our faith and a vital principle in our mission to the people of the sea. They come at the end of long voyages and delight in a welcome to a strange country, with the chance to have a conversation that stretches beyond on-board chatter. We listen to them and the stories they are keen to tell, mostly about their loved ones at home.

The other call of mission that applies here is

Go to where the hurt is.

I hear that phrase in all that Pope Francis calls us to do. He refers to our place of ministry as 'the Field Hospital.'

The field hospital is not bothered about its status or privileges. It is not concerned with targets or best practice indicators. Instead, it goes out of itself to respond to the needs of those whose lives are at risk. It goes to where people hurt, to be with them in that broken place.

And surely this idea of the field hospital is very much a model for our ministry. We go to where the hurt is, to where people are wounded, vulnerable or exploited. We do it all the time and don't wait until the time is right. We don't wait until specialist help is available. We get on with it in whatever way we can.

We do this in response to the call of Jesus in the

Gospels and to the guiding teachings of the Church where we are asked to respond to those in need. In his final discourse to the disciples in Matthew's Gospel 25, Jesus says;

> *I was hungry, and you gave me food, thirsty and you gave me drink. I was a stranger, and you made me welcome, lacking clothes and you clothed me, sick and you visited me, in prison and you came to see me.*

We do all of these things on a daily basis. But whatever we do, we do it in the context of a church agency bringing the joy of the gospel into a world that cries out in pain for the many injustices perpetrated against its people.

The first branch of what would ultimately become Stella Maris was set up in 1920 in Glasgow. The group's intent was to visit ships and distribute Catholic literature, but also to provide facilities for Catholic seafarers to use. Many were hostels or houses with up to 100 beds so that seafarers could live there between contracts at sea, and some provided evening facilities.

Sailors' contracts ended as soon as they were signed off, and ship owners would not want to pay them while the dock workers were unloading and then reloading, which could take anything up to a few weeks. The seafarer would stay in the centre between voyages—even if they were travelling out on the same ship they came in on.

As time passed and practices changed, the residential centres became under-used. It became clear that the focus of the mission had to change, and so the residential centres were closed. The various sections of the charity came together to form one unified whole, more focussed on ship-board mission than centres on land. The involvement of lay chaplaincy allowed an increase in ship visits, and chaplaincy training courses that included ship operations and port safety practices were made available.

A large percentage of the world's seafarers are Filipinos, and another great Catholic tranche comes from southern India. There is a real hunger for the Eucharist and the crews love to have mass celebrated on board their ship. This usually happens in the mess room; the place where the crew share their food becomes the focal point for the Eucharist. At Communion time, I go out onto the deck and engine room to distribute the sacred hosts, so that those working are not left out.

We offer a ministry of welcome to everyone, regardless of faith or background, visiting an average six ships a day. Some twenty will dock in Immingham and around fifty across the entire extent of the South Humberside patch: Boston, Sutton Bridge and New Holland are other ports of call, with our ship-visitor volunteers providing crucial support.

Stella Maris prides itself as a charity focused on people of all faiths or indeed no faith. The charity certainly does not proselytise but treats all individuals with equal respect. Chinese, Thai and Muslim seafarers all get visits from our chaplains and I take great pride in that mission of diversity.

Over 11,000 seafarers from across the world visited the Immingham Seafarers' Centre last year. Away from home for up to twelve months, here they can Skype loved ones, pick up a book from the library, or enjoy a relaxing beer.

Today Stella Maris has 200 port chaplains active in 314 ports worldwide across 55 countries, including the Port of Immingham. It is the premier ship-visiting charity around the world.

Even the name 'Stella Maris' has acquired a great degree of recognition.

On many occasions when I board ships, even before I've had a chance to introduce myself, a seafarer will notice the emblem on my jacket and enthuse joyfully "Ah, Stella Maris!" It's as if he knows immediately that he is being visited by someone who will understand the world he inhabits and can be trusted at all levels.

Crew are reluctant to make complaints, no matter how serious their grievances. They fear they may be sent home or even blacklisted, never to work on a ship again. But somehow they trust that a Chaplain can bring resolution to problems, without ever having their name or rank brought into the equation.

Of course this puts a great responsibility on the visitor to live up to such expectations in pursuit of justice, but the charity's name itself requires some living up to.

'Star of the Sea' is a title given to our blessed Mother, who brings great joy and comfort to seafarers around the world. There is a bit of confusion as to the first use of the title.

It is generally ascribed to a copyist of the works of

Saint Jerome. Some consider 'stella' to be the mistake of someone who intended to write 'Stilla Maris' (drop of the sea), but it was written as 'Stella Maris' (star of the sea), and this transcription error became widespread.

How true this is we will never know, but the term has been around for a very long time. The hymn Ave Maris Stella was written in the eighth century.

(A few years ago I had a most enjoyable experience with an elderly Polish Captain who told me he could sing all seven verses of the hymn, and he did.)

St John ascribes the following words to Jesus in his last moments on the cross.

> *"Jesus said to his mother, 'Woman, this is your son.' Then to the disciple he said, 'This is your mother.' And from that hour the disciple took her into his home."* (John 19:27.)

It is clear from some images in mess rooms and cabins that many seafarers take these words to heart. It is common on ships with Catholic crew to see a statue of Stella Maris on the bridge, usually behind the wheel. I've had occasions when preparing to celebrate Mass onboard to find the altar laid out with images of Our Lady, rosaries and the Stella Maris statue. As one Captain said to me, "This is our guidance."

I suppose all of us will have a favourite piece of scripture where Mary features. The Annunciation, the Nativity and the wedding at Cana are widely read and bring comfort to many, but for me the Magnificat is a favourite one. When I pray it onboard with crew or as a part of the office in the Mission chapel, it becomes apparent how the words resonate with the experience of seafarers who often feel themselves as 'the lowly' waiting in hope to be raised up.

In Luke 1. 46-55 Mary is no longer a silent, obedient and compliant girl but a young woman singing a song about toppling rulers from their thrones, echoing the words of Hannah (1 Sam. 2). This young pregnant girl recalls the great deeds the Lord has done for his people and expresses the hope that the Lord will do the same again for his oppressed people.

> *He has used the power of his arm.*
>
> *He has routed the arrogant of heart.*
>
> *He has pulled down princes from their thrones and raised up the lowly.*
>
> *He has filled the starving with good things and sent the rich away empty.*
>
> Luke 1. 51-53

Poor and oppressed people often identify with this song—the longest set of words spoken by a woman in the New Testament. Dietrich Bonhoeffer, a German theologian who was executed by the Nazis, called the Magnificat "the most passionate, the wildest hymn ever sung."

But it would be a shallow interpretation of Luke to see this prayer as that of a faithful young girl declaring her faith in a loving God who will overturn an unfavourable world order. It is that, but at the same time Mary is coming to terms with a new power within herself. She has a new sense of the Lord being inside her, giving her the strength to allow the Lord to do great things through her.

I often wonder if we really understand the greatness of God that is within us. Far too often we sense we plough a lone furrow, thinking that things can only happen through our own strengths and talents. That's when we fail. The great mystic Julian of Norwich expresses this so well.

> "Greatly ought we to rejoice that God dwells in our soul; and more greatly ought we to rejoice that our soul dwells in God. Our soul is created to be God's dwelling place, and the dwelling of our soul is God."
>
> Revelations of Divine Love, c. 1373

Infinite love is planted within the soul of all humans and all of creation. It is vital that chaplains understand their ministry as something beyond the 'doing'. They need to understand the great love of God that fills their souls, and the souls of those to whom they speak. God's power within us should help us bring the joy of the Gospel to seafarers who are the oppressed ones in this cruel globalised world of shipping.

And so our Stella Maris is pre-eminently the Mother of the poor and downtrodden, those with little say or influence. As the Polish Captain sang to me,

Break the captives' fetters,
Light on blindness pour,
All our ills expelling,
Every bliss implore.
Ave Maris Stella, 8th century hymn, Anon

4

A SEA OF MANY LANGUAGES

When I give talks about my work, one of the most asked questions is, "How do you manage with language?"

I'm ashamed to say my language skills are pitiful and I harbour a great regret that I didn't pursue language subjects at school and beyond. My 'O' level in Gaelic has been of no use whatsoever in the seafaring world!

I wandered into the library one night and met a Russian seafarer browsing along the shelves. "Are you looking for anything in particular?" I asked, just by way of conversation.

"Great Expectations. Do you know if you have it?"

I pointed him to the section of non-English-language books.

"No, thank you. I read it in Russian at school; now I'd like to read it in English."

English is the communication language of the sea so most seafarers have a good command of the language, especially the younger ones. An exception to this would be Chinese crew: officers have to speak English, but the ratings haven't quite got there yet. Generally on a ship there will be someone with whom we can communicate; but in a time of tragedy, lack of communication is a dreadful barrier.

I received a message from the Harbour Master that I needed to get to a large coal carrier that was just berthing at Immingham. He told me there had been an accident onboard.

When I got there, I saw one of those sights that unfortunately will stay with me forever. About twenty Chinese crew were screaming and crying, stood around the body of one of their own, lying in a pool of blood. I'm sure they didn't even know what country they were in, not that that mattered at the time.

The lad had let the steel line cable out to the tug aft of their ship, but when a connection was made, the cable snapped and flew back to the ship to hit him in the head fatally.

So there I am, on a ship full of Chinese men in great distress. I am called to the scene as a chaplain, but what do I do?

It's not the kind of thing you are prepared for in your training and that's one of the scary/exciting things about chaplaincy to the people of the sea. You just never know and have to be prepared for any contingency.

I happened to have a bunch of UK SIM cards with me

so I gave one to each crew-member and, through the Captain, told them to go to a quiet part of the ship and speak to a loved one back home.

What would you have done? Maybe cry with them? That would not have been a bad thing.

5
_____

LIFE OF SEAFARERS

I call the world of shipping 'an invisible world'. You see, the work of seafarers is vital to every aspect of how we live, and yet the lives of the people who bring all this to us remain a mystery. I've also heard it referred to as 'sea-blindness'.

It may be invisible, but shame on us if we were ever to take it for granted. And more so if we were never to give a thought to the crews of the ships who work in a harsh, dangerous and sometimes cruel environment.

A seafarer is generally on contract for about nine months. That means working every day, usually six hours on, six off. The crew is generally pretty well looked after with regard to food and salary. About eighty percent of their salary is paid into the family bank at home, and the rest is kept in the Master's safe as spending money when they arrive in port. It is a hard life and lacks many of the basic comforts that we take for granted.

One of my first visits on a ship opened my eyes to my naïvety. I met a Filipino man in the messroom, cases packed all ready to go home after ten months at sea. I said,

"How joyful you must be feeling knowing you will soon see your wife and two young children!"

He smiled at my short-sightedness. "It will be very difficult for the first few weeks. My children will not know me, and will see me as an intruder coming into a family that has been living their own way. They will cry, almost in fear of the stranger, before they get to  know and understand who I am. No sooner do they get used to me than there will be more tears, as I say goodbye to them for another long voyage." He sighed. "One day they will understand."

Much can happen in family life when a loved one is at sea. A child may be born and the seafarer's first sighting of them may be via Skype when finally ashore. I've witnessed a husband and wife naming their child via Skype.

One evening I noticed a Russian seafarer sitting alone in a dark corner of our centre. Getting closer I could hear him singing very quietly, and he beckoned me to join him where I could see that he was singing his newborn son to sleep. That was their first meeting.

On the other hand, I have sometimes sat with a seaman who has just come ashore after a long voyage, when the much anticipated conversation brought news of a family death. It is difficult enough to deal with a death in real time, but how do you grieve retrospectively?

And though it is difficult enough in the best of situations, less favourable situations are all too frequent. Too many seafarers, from the developing world in particular, are confined and intimidated on board ship. The shipping roads are virtually impossible to police, and hence virtually lawless. They are wage slaves, enduring injustice and indignity but living in dread of blacklisting and consequent privations for their families back home. (People-trafficking and enslavement are even occurring in the merchant and shipping fleets).

While the appropriate authorities can and do intervene, the port chaplain has a unique and trusted role. They must be someone the seafarers can safely talk to, who actually might be inclined to—and able to—help them. But it is necessary to really understand port life in order to do so. In this marginal and murky world, the worst outcome would be to handle it badly and end up making the seafarers' lives worse.

On the other hand, we can support them in many other ways, and we do. Seafarers treasure their rosary beads and as chaplains we are often asked to supply them. The rosary seems to be a prayer that suits them especially when on duty, for they can recite the Hail Marys and Our Fathers while doing other things.

Last year I had a chat with Ronald, a regular visitor to our port. He told me he recites three mysteries of the Rosary each day.

"Do you have a favourite?" I asked.

"The sorrowful mysteries," he said. "When I finish them, I realise things can't get any worse." An unusual answer, but I think I know what he means.

It would be cheap and easy to dismiss such things as pious or superstitious nonsense, but the reality is quite different.

6

THE IMMINGHAM FLOOD

On December 5, 2013, the greatest tidal surge in sixty years caused havoc along the U.K.'s East Coast. The Humber, and in particular the Port of Immingham, bore the brunt of it. It was a day I will always remember, and I know I'm not alone in that. We all have vivid memories of the water engulfing our port, of vehicles floating around carparks and the lights going out; there was an unprecedented crisis unfolding around us.

Sited in one of the lowest-lying parts of the port, our Seafarers' Centre was overwhelmed in the tidal surge, and what had been a haven, a place of peace and community, became a wreck in a matter of minutes.

I was devastated when I saw it for the first time following the flood. The place was destroyed but, not only that, it was as if all the joy and the happiness that the building had seen over the years had been completely washed away by the silty water.

It caused thousands of pounds' worth of damage to our Seafarers' Centre, which was forced to close for nine months. We lost around 1500 donated festive boxes filled with toiletries, socks, jerseys, and colourful knitted bonnets, intended as Christmas gifts for seafarers far from home. Pool tables, ping-pong tables and the entire shop stock were washed away.

The chapel too met a similar fate, the chairs and the small altar floating in four foot of stinking silt and sea water. Even the vehicles used by the Chaplains to bring seafarers ashore were destroyed—everything was ruined.

I live in a little bedsit 'above the shop' on the first floor of the Centre and stayed in the building throughout the refurbishment, despite dire warnings about the dangers of spores and lack of heat. I was determined to be there to welcome the 'pilgrims' on their return; the building might be in ruin, but our mission continued.

The only other part of the building still functioning was a small office on the first floor. I remember it as a refuelling centre where the fridge was always stocked with drinks and chocolate. There Ros, the Centre Manager, planned the reordering of the centre. It was her vision that took a ruined building and restored it to create the finest Seafarer Centre in the UK. Her time was divided between keeping workmen to the task in hand, and linking me to seafarers who rang in for help.

We became a mobile mission; my minibus was stuffed full of computers and mobile internet connection devices, SIM cards, toiletries and chocolate—all the things that the seafarers would have found at the Centre. We took internet connections to the ships and kept replenishing them with credit.

In the days that followed, a team of dock workers removed everything from the building and cleared out the mud and filth left by the surge. They tore down doors, skirting boards, cables and ceilings, and threw them in skips. For days the din of large hammers was all that could be heard, and the dock workers were not subtle—that is, until they began to clear the chapel.

Here they showed a reverence that really took me by surprise. They took a more gentle approach; even the hammer blows sounded less threatening. They insisted that I stay with them throughout the "reorganisation" of the room. Nothing was touched without my say-so. The statue of the Madonna and Child was on a plinth above the water level, but the foreman was embarrassed to tell me that even she had to go, according to their instructions.

"No, she stays to oversee the rebuild," I insisted.

For the next nine months, that statue sat by the bread bin in my little kitchen above the ruin, while below, seventeen industrial drying machines ran flat out twenty-four hours a day for four whole months to dry the building, after which the refurbishment and redecorating could begin.

But when it did, the Centre was not just brought back to its previous state, but improved massively, as local organisations and charities who had heard about it in the news raised funds to create an even better facility.

At the beginning of September 2014, the refurbished

Centre finally reopened. The Madonna and Child moved back down from my bread bin and now sit on a new plinth in the beautifully restored chapel. The new Centre includes a smart café bar serving hot food and drinks, free WiFi communication throughout the centre, large TV screens, a games room with table tennis, table football and a pool table, and much more besides. The Centre also has a new fifteen-seater minibus.

John Fitzgerald, director of the Association of British Ports, had this to add. "The destruction of the Centre felt like the soul of the port had been broken," he said. "It provides an extraordinary service for these unsung heroes but, as Colum and his team have demonstrated, out of the ashes opportunities arise, and this new and improved Centre offers even better facilities for our visiting friends. The staff here, and many other businesses and individuals including ABP, made sure that was possible, and the opening was full of exhilaration and joy. The UK's number one port now has the UK's number one Seafarers' Centre."

The tidal surge caused a huge amount of damage and distress, but it also demonstrated what an incredible group of people work in our port. One of the great lessons in this is that Church and Church Mission does not depend on buildings. The mission of outreach to the stranger continued and inspired even more volunteers to come along to help us.

7
_____

PERSPECTIVE

So there you are, you're having a good old rant; you're on a roll, desperate to convince whoever you get to listen that life is so unfair. Your misery knows no bounds. And don't you just hate it when they turn to you and say, "I think maybe you should get this in perspective"?

Perspective? I don't want to put things in perspective. I want the world to know how life has treated me badly. I want sympathy…

At its core, perspective is the way we see the world and our place in it. A healthy perspective grounds us in the reality of what is; it recognises who we are and how we are fit in the world. It allows us to better interact and relate to others, and it judges freely how to proceed based on a balanced vision of experiences and encounters.

Perspective, of course, comes from our own vantage point. Thus, to have a balanced and fairly realistic view both of what has been and what is, requires self-awareness, frank honesty, deep patience and a willingness to consider the many sides of a situation. Gaining perspective, then, is a process that requires the hard work of mindfulness, which ultimately leads to peace.

This work of gaining perspective is done both in our everyday interactions and in the silence of our hearts. A healthy perspective

"doesn't only see what we wish to see ... it allows us to better encounter everything we must face to move forward in life," psychologist Dr Robert Wicks writes. "[A healthy perspective] doesn't help us run away from the truth ... it enables us to put things in their proper place."

PERSPECTIVE: THE CALM WITHIN THE STORM,
ROBERT WICKS 2014

But when perspective is lost, the real world, where there is so much seriously wrong, gets blotted out. Contentment gives way to restlessness, things get out of focus and small irritants can become major crises.

If you are anything like me, you have a handful of difficulties or problems lurking in your brain at any one time. They can be minor irritants like why the bus isn't on time, or worries about the busy day ahead. And then we have the big ones like coping with ailing parents, issues with our children, marriage problems, or job loss.

Of course we worry and we fret.

I know. It happens to me all the time. I too keep losing perspective and become obsessed with something l cannot have, with hurts that I cannot let go of… And then I fail to notice what's around me in this cruel world. I spend too many hours stewing about old hurts, replaying again and again what someone said, insults and misunderstandings that have come my way, and dwelling on the unfairness of life.

What do I need to do?

Maybe I need to appreciate the present and take life moment by moment, rather than worrying about what was or what will be.

So the next time someone stops you in mid rant and tells you to put things in perspective, don't get defensive. Pause and think about it—they maybe be doing you a favour.

After the flood at Immingham, I was really struck by the devastation it caused and our recovery from it. One of my friends commented on how much I talked about it.

I laughed. "Have you not been warned about the port chaplain?"

"What do you mean?" he asked.

"Well, they say of Father Colum that wherever he goes, the story of The Great Flood of Immingham Dock goes with him. He tells it wherever there is a semblance of interest from the listeners, and even if there isn't, it doesn't matter. The story is told in bars, cafes, and even to complete strangers who hadn't anticipated their day being interrupted by this strange man and his story. Nothing can deter him! I tell you, he'll be telling it right up to the day he's called to meet his Maker."

"Goodness!" My friend did not quite know what to make of this.

"At the gates St Peter will say, 'Welcome! Come in! You can introduce yourself to the great heavenly assembly tomorrow,'" I went on, "and Father Colum will reply 'Wonderful, I will tell them of the Great Flood of Immingham December 2013. They'll never have heard anything like it; the power of the wave surge, the utter destruction and devastation.'"

My friend leaned over conspiratorially. "And you know what St Peter will say, don't you?"

"No..." I replied warily.

A mischievous grin spread across his face. "St Peter will say, 'OK, you can tell them, but I should warn you—Noah will be sat in the front row...'!"

8

THE THINGS WE TAKE FOR GRANTED...

Language can be a tricky obstacle to deal with, but the reality is that most seafarers who come our way speak very good English. One evening I wandered to the shop in the Centre to find an elderly Ukrainian gentleman becoming exasperated that the lady there couldn't make out what he needed.

He kept trying to explain, but whatever it was, it sounded a bit like 'benium'. Being very clever about these things, I took him across to where the medicines were stacked. I showed him a tube of Bonjella for the painful gums he didn't have. And then Benylin for the cough he didn't have...

His exasperation was beginning to be tinged with a bit of anger and one of the younger crew from his ship came over to see if he could help.

"Do you know what 'benium' is?" I asked.

"No, but I will ask him." He spoke to the elderly gentleman to see what he really wanted, then laughed.

"What was it?" I asked.

"A 'Boney M' CD," the younger man told me.

"Now why didn't I think of that?!" I asked. He laughed and went away.

Asking the gentleman to wait, I went upstairs to my flat and got him a CD of Bony M's greatest hits. He went away smiling and very happy. I'm sure he told the story many times of the strange people in the Seafarer Centre who thought he had a cough and bad gums, but hopefully he enjoyed the CD at least!

I've heard some great stories of how some of the older men have learnt their bit of English. George, a Polish engineer, came to our port every two months and was a regular visitor to our seafarer centre. I sat with him one evening and asked him how he had learnt to speak English.

"At school we sang English nursery rhymes," he announced, and went on to demonstrate his grasp of 'My Bonny Lies Over The Ocean' loudly. As a teenager he had been a big fan of Helen Shapiro and was proud to have taught himself the words of 'Walking Back To Happiness'.

I slipped away and downloaded the tune, then played it over our sound system. He sang along though tearfully and gave me a big hug. I often think of George, now certainly retired, and wish him an abundance of that happiness.

As I often say to chaplains and volunteers "Never underestimate the value of the small gesture." Sometimes it can be something and nothing, something that we would take for granted: but many things that are everyday to us can mean the world to a seafarer. What do I mean by 'the things we take for granted'?

In this 'instant' society everything seems to be at hand for us; our remote controls so we don't have to leave our armchairs, our ability to text and tweet or join in the latest communication fad.

It's hard to even remember a time without mobile phones. Now they've become an everyday attachment, we take it for granted that almost everyone has one.

"What's your mobile number?" we are constantly being asked. We talk about loving to get away from the phone on holiday, even…

Instant communication is all around us, but it's a luxury seafarers do not have. How strange that in this hi-tech age seafarers can only communicate with their families in the time they are allowed ashore! Not for them the luxury of instant chat while away at sea, or the joy of a text message from a loved one. Often at sea on nine-month contracts, it can be weeks or months before they catch up on the latest family news. They can be months at sea without contact with their families.

So in our Seafarers' Centres around the country we provide telephones and computers to help the men keep in touch with their loved ones. Of course this can be a great joy, but it is often tinged with the sadness at the limitation of that contact.

The calls don't always bring good news. Just recently, a

young lad came out of one of our phone boxes sobbing and crying his eyes out. He had just called home, after a month at sea, to be told his mother, Flora, had died suddenly. Of course there was no question of returning home to join with other family members in their grief, and Thomas was back on duty that evening, the companionship of his shipmates his only comfort.

Next day I was asked by the Captain to celebrate a requiem mass on board for Flora. We all signed a card to be kept in her memory and, at least in some small way, Thomas was able to share his grief amongst friends.

Webcams can bring the seafarer closer to home, for at least he can see his family and talk almost face to face. I often walk around our communication room sharing the simple joy of being invited to "wave to my wife" or "say hello to my son". Just last evening Ronald was sat staring intently at the screen, just watching his child sleeping... The things we take for granted.

There was great excitement last month when a crew gathered round a screen to be with Paul as he saw his newborn baby for the first time. There was happiness all around and Paul and his wife talked about names for their child; they named him Joseph. One of our volunteers went out to buy a cake, and we all celebrated for the short time that was left of their trip ashore.

So the next time you feel angry at the endless ringing of your phones, spare a thought for the lads at sea, who would love to have the luxury of a call from home.

9

CARGO OF LOVE

When a ship arrives to discharge its cargo, we as chaplains and ship visitors go on board bringing our own particular cargo to the visiting crew. That cargo might be in the form of phone cards, or internet lines to connect them to family. It might be in sacramental form when Mass or Holy Communion can be celebrated; maybe some extra luxuries that we are able to bring directly because of the generosity of your support.

Whatever form it takes, I have begun to think of it as a 'cargo of love'. Why? Let me explain.

A few months ago, we had a very sad crew arrive in Immingham. As the ship had been leaving Rotterdam, one of the lads had an accident. The young man fell to his death and his friends watched in horror as his body was washed away. (Sadly, this is a thing that happens relatively often in the world of shipping, but it never gets any easier to deal with.)

In a matter of seconds, the lives of Benjy's family and friends had changed forever. The crew would be haunted for a long time by what they had witnessed, and we can only begin to imagine the torment of his family back home. It is unlikely his family would ever even retrieve his body. The heartache was indescribable.

I went onboard and over the course of a few days I spoke with the crew, celebrated Mass in Benjy's memory, said prayers for his family, blessed his cabin and did what you would expect of a port chaplain.

But then something special happened. Two of our lady ship-visitors, who had heard of the tragedy, baked loads of cakes and brought them onboard. The joy that came about from that simple act was almost miraculous. They had brought with them a cargo of love that I could never have even dreamt of.

The sister ship arrived in the port a week later, and I went on board as usual. But all the lads wanted to know was, "Will the ladies with the cakes be coming to visit?" Of course, they would be doing.

Yet again I was struck by the power of volunteer support. On what was a very sad occasion, I had done everything that could have been expected of me as a chaplain, and hoped I had done it well. They did something more, and that thing done in love brought a transformation that I could never have achieved.

I told this story a year later to a group of chaplains at their national conference in Mauritius. The general feeling was that the efforts of two wonderful ladies highlighted something about our chaplaincy—the little extra. For the rest of the week, 'La Plus' became the byword for service.

There is something about what we do that thankfully appeals to people's generosity. There seem to be so many calls from more and more charities these days. Maybe the needs are greater or more clearly publicised. For whatever reason, there is a growing awareness of the plight of modern seafarers, and for that we are grateful. This generosity is expressed in many forms:

-Direct monetary donations: for instance, in our annual Sea Sunday appeal in the UK Churches.

-Donations of clothing, as the crews who visit us are often from hot countries and come ill-prepared for a cold wet winter.

-Donations of time. It is so reassuring to find volunteers, either trained ship visitors, or parish supporters who give of their precious time to help in what we do.

We receive hundreds of woolly hats, for this is practically part of the uniform of a seafarer. People create these colourful items either as individuals or part of knitting groups. The seafarers call them their bonnets and like to have new ones, almost for every trip. New voyage, new bonnet.

Volunteers play a major role in the work of Stella Maris in the ports and in the parishes, and without them our work would diminish in so many ways. In ports around the world, visitors work alongside chaplains to enrich the work of mission to the people of the sea.

Let me say a word about the wonderful team of ship visitors in the port of Immingham, not because there are no quality teams in other ports (there are), but I obviously know the Grimsby team and the work they do.

When I joined Stella Maris (then known as The Apostleship of the Sea or AoS) in 2004, the work of the visitors was just beginning to be understood and developed. It had really taken off and been developed in the Tees ports around 2003 under the leadership of Tony McAvoy, the port chaplain. Tony brought his team to share their experiences with a group of potential volunteers from Grimsby and Immingham. They made a big impression, and there was a feeling that we should get on with making something like that begin in the Humber ports.

It was my job to get on the road to encourage people into this great ministry. I spoke in churches, schools, group gatherings, in fact wherever I could, to get people interested. There was already a buzz in the air, especially in local parishes, that this great ministry was being carried out within their parish boundaries.

I stressed in all my talks that I didn't want people to volunteer simply to help a busy chaplain. I emphasised the importance of their Baptism which made them sharers in the priesthood of Christ and now called them to share in this great ministry of outreach to the stranger. That chance might never come their way again.

So I invited people to come and see. Some spent a day or two with a chaplain, visiting ships and talking to crew. Once they decided that this might be a good thing to get involved with at this particular time in life, serious training began. Merchant Navy Welfare Board is an umbrella for maritime charities and provides various training modules for those who wish to become *bona fide* visitors. Stella Maris provides safety wear and insurance for all volunteers. The volunteers must know how valued their contribution is to the great mission of the church.

When I speak to chaplains around the world, they all talk of the importance of the volunteers who support the work of mission.

10

NO LITURGICAL SEASONS AT SEA

Where two or three meet in my name, I am there among them.
(Matt 18:20)

Liturgical seasons aren't really catered for in the seafaring world. At sea, Easter and Christmas will be celebrated perhaps within a month of the dates we celebrate on land. The Easter season is a special time for seafarers where they like to combine Ash Wednesday, Palm Sunday, Holy Thursday, Good Friday and Easter Sunday. Invariably they like to be marked with ashes, receive a palm cross and hopefully combine Easter Mass with the reception of chocolate eggs. A nightmare for the Liturgical experts, I'm sure.

Christmas Mass is very important to the crew, and it is a real privilege for me to be able to celebrate this great feast for them, irrespective of the precise date. A crew leaving here in early to mid-December is likely to be at sea for Christmas and even if in a port, it is unlikely that a priest will be found to celebrate Mass for the crew on Christmas Day itself.

Masses are celebrated on board or in our Centre chapel

and this year around four hundred seafarers have rejoiced in the Christmas story through Mass.

Scripture offers us a splendid list of places associated with the Christmas story, such as Nazareth, Bethlehem, Jerusalem, Egypt and Syria. However, for me, Christmas begins each year in the unlikely setting of Woodall Service station on the M1. It is there that I meet a group of parishioners from St Patrick's parish in Leicester and the extraordinary arrival of the Christmas shoeboxes begins.

Later, shoeboxes stuffed with little luxury items arrive from other parishes and schools in the diocese, notably from Cleethorpes, Grimsby and Lincoln. Boxes also arrive from parishes in Leeds, Sheffield, Selby and Coventry; in all this year we presented 1200 shoeboxes to seafarers and around 200 smaller gift packages—a tremendous act of giving.

I remember vividly when the idea first came to us. A ship with an Italian crew came to the port, and I made what seemed a fairly routine visit. The crew was particularly quiet, but I put that down to the long voyage they had just endured. I told them about our wonderful Centre and that if they wished, a bus would bring them to celebrate Mass in the chapel. All was agreed, and a time was set, but that evening I noticed that not one member of the crew had come ashore.

I went back to the ship to see if some problem had arisen. It was then the Chief Mate told me they couldn't come ashore; no one had any money. The crew had not been paid for four months and basic provisions were dangerously low. He said they had no toiletries. "There's not even a bar of soap on the ship."

I asked him to get as many crew as possible to come to the Centre and told him all would be provided. Once there, we gave each one a shopping basket to fill with all they wanted. Toiletries and chocolate seemed to be the prize items, and they went back to the ship happy for the present.

All was paid for by what I refer to as 'the angels of the hour'. There is always someone whose generosity rises to the occasion; I have found this so often in my years of service to Stella Maris, and that night was no exception.

A few of us decided to make an appeal in local parishes for Christmastime. People would be asked to add a few things to their weekly shopping, and we would collect them and wrap them up as Christmas presents for visiting crew. I knew that this was being done in various ports around the country and saw no reason why it couldn't work for us.

And how it worked!

The first year we gave out about eighty shoeboxes, but that has snowballed; now we give out more than a thousand every Christmas.

Seafarers have little chance of receiving anything from their companies, so how wonderful that the Catholic communities make their mark in such generous style.

I brought twenty two boxes to an Indian crew on board a bulk carrier, one year.

The Chief Mate asked me, "Where does it all come from?"

I explained that all is provided by our parish communities.

He said, "Such generosity—and for people they will never meet."

Again that word *generosity*; we depend so much on that. I was asked once, "Why do you have this shoebox appeal? Surely seafarers already have most things that go into the boxes."

"Yes, most of them do," I answered, "but isn't it a lovely thing to receive a present, something to open on Christmas Day, wherever you are in the world? And how many times do we get a present of something of which we have an abundance? Where would we be without the Christmas socks or eyeliner….?"

I often wondered what happened on the ship on Christmas Day at sea, and when the boxes got opened. When I asked various crews on their return, they all told the same story.

If the ship is quiet after lunch, the Captain arranges the crew in a circle and they open the boxes, one by one, making a big thing of each item to make the occasion last longer. Is there anything special about a new comb or toothbrush or some smellies? There is, when it is lovingly wrapped and may be the only sign that you are remembered at this special time of year.

One year, just when I thought that most of the Christmas work had been done, a routine ship visit on New Year's Eve raised a whole new scenario.

The ship had brought a cargo of biomass from Canada. I was welcomed as usual, and the Captain told me that he had been praying for a visit from a priest ever since they set sail on their maiden voyage four months previously. The ship needed to be blessed and the chance to have Christmas Mass on board as well was indeed many blessings all at once.

So on New Year's Day I went onboard with twenty shoeboxes and went to the mess room to set up for Mass. The room had been transformed and, with the exception of three crew on essential cover, all were present. It was a best jumper day, and throughout Mass the crew sang carols from their printed sheets.

After Mass we began the ship-blessing. I assumed a new ship would have a lift—but not this one. As the years go by, my once fit and flexible knees complain regularly. Steep gangways and towers are not ideal for ancient knees, and on this ship there were a lot of stairs to contend with! First, we went down to the engine room. I normally say a blessing prayer from the top level, but this Captain wanted all eight floors to be blessed. Then a thirteen-floor climb to the bridge, followed by a visit to bless the galley for the cook, followed by the ship's office and finally the mess room.

The Captain had laid on a very special lunch for all the crew to complete a perfect celebration, and this is not something that normally happens. It was a real red-letter day for all concerned.

I am ever humbled by the response I receive from a crew when I am simply doing something that is an everyday part of my life. 'Hunger for Eucharist' is a nice phrase that I have heard many times in parish life, but I have not fully understood the reality of this until I encountered the world of seafaring. Eucharist can be a daily event in parish life, but for a seafarer, away from home and church for many months, this is a rare occurrence—indeed, a real celebration.

However, many of our chaplains do hold services of Holy Communion on ships when a priest is not available. They are commissioned by their local parish, where they are usually extraordinary ministers of the Eucharist. This too brings great joy to Catholic crew, who experience a connection with the Church wherever they may be in the world.

This is what makes Stella Maris special, getting to the heart of the spiritual needs of a crew. We do it in many ways, but once in a while something like this happens, and you realise how much our service is valued.

11

A DRY BOND

The time between Christmas and New Year can be a bleak period in any major port. Lots of people are still off work, and ships are anchored in the bay, avoiding port fees until everything gets back into some semblance of normality. And that bleakness hits new heights on the small wharf jetties. The small ships are generally laying against the riverbank at the mercy of the tides.

That's where we found a ship tilted about thirty degrees to port. It looked like a drunk holding himself up at the bar when his legs could no longer be trusted. The drunk image was heightened by a bunch of empties alongside on the bank. Vodka, gin, brandy and many other bottles, now abandoned and embedded in the late December ice. As we went for a closer look, six Filipino crew came to greet us, delighted that we were from Stella Maris and might be able to help them.

The story took us into another level of bleakness. The only other member of the crew was the Captain who, we were assured, was asleep in his cabin as he had been for the entire voyage and stopover. He had a particular liking for the liquid stuff of the ship's bond and often drank it dry.

Bond regulations are complex and regularly under review in the shipping world. The bond safe can only legally be opened while in international waters, and in each destination port a declaration form is completed and given to the ship's agent who can submit it to the local authorities upon request.

Recently the ship entered a North European port and was subject to a routine inspection by Customs and Excise Officers. They were not happy to find the bond safe empty. A dry bond with no records or receipts meant the immediate imposition of a hefty fine.

Each cabin was searched and nothing untoward was found there. The crew signed a customs declaration to say they each had a bottle of spirits to which they were entitled for the journey.

Carlos, the boswain, took up the story.

"We were all called to the bridge and were told we were to be fined £10,000. The Captain said we would share out the fine, and despite objections from the six of us that we had nothing to do with the problem, the Customs team left the ship and told us to settle the matter with the shipowner."

The company fined all of them £1300, which was taken from their wage with the result that their families had no money over Christmas.

I'm sure you can imagine the families' horror to discover that no money had been paid into their bank accounts that month—and at such a time of year. To make it worse, no communication is possible while at sea, so the crew knew nothing of this until they arrived in our port on Boxing Day and received frantic calls from loved ones.

It was no surprise, therefore, to find them in such a state in the bleakness of that river bank. They were broken and wanted help, and of course, justice.

Later that day, I was able to contact a friendly, Christmas-spirited representative of the company.

"The crew all signed a customs declaration to say they had four bottles in their cabins," she assured me.

"I know for a fact that this is not the case," I told her, and argued for the men.

She looked again at the forms. "I think I know what has happened… The figure on the form is blurred and difficult to read. It looks like a four, so when they had been submitted to the company, that's how it was read—but looking at it now, I think you are right that the figure is a one."

"What can we do to sort this out?"

We discussed it a bit further, and I returned to the ship that night to see the crew before they sailed the following morning. I was able to tell them that a company agent would visit the ship on arrival at the next port and put the matter right—or as right as it could be, considering what the crew and their families had suffered through no fault of their own.

I have been asked many times what is so different from my work in mission in the shipping world and that in a typical parish.

In a parish you follow the story. You help a family and follow their story as long as you stay in that community. Even when you move to a new posting, communication is easy, and the history is ongoing. In the shipping world you can help a crew in a major way, but the ship sails and you may never find out how the story ended. On this occasion, however, I did.

About a month later, the same crew sailed into Immingham and the men came to see me. They filled me in with the details of how that story ended—and what an amazing ending!

The representative of the shipping company did visit them on their arrival in Hamburg and apologised for their distress. Their docked wages were immediately restored, with a small bonus added. Of course, this could never make up for the situation at home where Christmas had been a time of some distress for the families of the six. The Captain was severely reprimanded for not correcting the figures and, they suspected, received a huge fine.

What they told me next humbled me in a way I will never forget. When it was then put to the crew that the Captain would be sacked for causing them so much distress, they pleaded on his behalf, "No. We forgive him."

I know that in scripture we are told time and time again about the importance of forgiveness, but in those circumstances could you forgive? I have thought many times of their brave decision. How could they forgive so much hurt that had been piled upon them and their loved ones? Of course, the insistence of Jesus to Peter that he forgive not seven times but seventy-seven times is a lesson for us all. The words are there, but can we really take them off the page and put them into practice?

The great spiritual writers have a lot to say on this matter of forgiveness. It's not an option but an absolute necessity if we are to find peace within us. To carry around old wounds and even hatred for something someone may have done to us is self-destructive. On the other hand, to forgive another person from the heart is an act of liberation.

We free the one who has injured us from the things that have soured and broken our relationship. We also free ourselves from the burden of being the one who carries all the hurt. As long as we do not forgive those who have wounded us, we carry a toxic cargo that can eat away at our very being. Forgiveness, therefore, liberates not only the other person but also ourselves.

Indeed, real growth in the spiritual life demands we throw overboard old hurts and perceived grievances, and sail on, much lighter and fit for the voyage. So the memory of a bleak December will always be trumped by the words 'No, we forgive him.'

What a Christmas lesson for me!

12

CARGO

In such a busy port as Immingham, I see many ships every day. Coming or going, the thing they have in common is the utter need to have a cargo that is stored in balance. Even weight distribution, just enough fuel and food for the journey, and the right number of fit crew are all vital to ensure the journey can be made safely.

It got me thinking of the cargo we carry in our daily lives. We are all on journeys but just like the ship, we too have to maintain a balance—enough of what we need but nothing excessive to slow us down.

Think of getting to the airport to find out you have excess baggage and must either get rid of it or pay a penalty. But what about the excess baggage of our hearts or heads—old wounds, old hurts, or resentments? These are the very things that can become obsessions and bring us down or slow our progress.

So why not take a little time to check your cargo? Maybe it is time to offload something that should have been dumped a long time ago.

And you know what? It will make for a smoother journey.

13

CASINO

Chinese seafarers are now seen quite regularly in our port. With the exception of senior officers, they generally know little English.

But one day as I signed in to the watchman's book he began to speak to me and proved to be much more fluent than his crewmates.

"Are you a priest?" he asked.

"Yes, I am."

"A Catholic priest?"

"Yes."

With a shushhhh and finger over his lips he took me to the back of his little watch hut.

"I am a Catholic and I have been hoping to meet a Catholic priest on one of my voyages." He was frightened that any other crew member should discover his religious affiliation, so he spoke softly as he produced a crucifix from his pocket.

He spoke of his great love of Pope Francis.

"Chinese Catholics wonder if he will ever come to our country to bless us as he has in so many other parts of the world."

We talked a little longer and then he knelt to receive a blessing.

He stood again beaming. "Thank you, thank you. This is one of the greatest days of my life!"

How very humbling for me—I hadn't really done anything, but perhaps there was something I could do…

"When do you finish your watch?" I asked.

"I have another thirty minutes to go. Why?"

"Would you like me to take you for an afternoon trip?" I thought for a moment. "We could go to one of our beautiful churches and maybe meet some of the local parishioners, or anything you want."

"Yes please, I'd like to go on a trip." He beamed. "Take me to a casino!"

Ah, the assumptions we make...

14

CHAPLAINCY

I've often wondered why Jesus broke with God's long tradition of employing shepherds and chose fishermen instead. Have you ever thought about it?

Moses was a shepherd. David was a shepherd. Jacob was a shepherd. In Psalm 23, the most famous Psalm in the history of Psalms, David famously sang, 'The Lord is my shepherd.'

Scripture refers to God's people in a number of places as his flock or the sheep of his hand. And it's not as if shepherds can be relegated to the Old Testament era of human history. After all, it was shepherds tending their flocks by night who were first to hear the news of the birth of Jesus. Jesus even referred to himself as the 'Good Shepherd', telling an unforgettable parable about the importance of the one lost sheep from the herd of a hundred.

But when it comes to choosing his disciples, it seems the bulk of them were indeed fishermen. What was it about fishermen that Jesus saw as vital in the inauguration of the kingdom?

Shepherds often live in isolation but fishermen are not hermits. They are social people who work with others. It takes a team of spirited strong men to catch fish with large nets. If a fisherman does not learn to work with others he will not be successful. The successful fisherman must deal with boatmen and must compete with many others in the fish market. He is not a loner.

The shepherd is usually given an existing flock and maintains that flock in good fashion, but a fisherman, by nature, is more aggressive than a shepherd. He must go out to catch new fish every day. Fishermen must work in all kinds of weather or they will starve. A fisherman who avoids rainy days and stays at home will soon be bankrupt.

A shepherd MAINTAINS a flock, a fisherman SEARCHES for new shoals.

In our church today, every member is called to be a fisherman, the one who searches for the new. Fishing becomes a form of evangelisation, not just maintenance.

In Stella Maris, we have great affection and admiration for the life of St Peter Claver. After ordination he lived and ministered in Cartagena, Columbia. It was a hub in the slave trade where Africans were traded; it is difficult to envisage a more dehumanising experience. St Peter didn't wait for people to come to him, for many were unable to do so. He would head for the wharf as soon as a slave ship entered the port. Boarding the ship, he entered the filthy and diseased holds to treat and minister to their badly treated, terrified human cargo, who had survived a voyage of several months under horrible conditions.

The workplace of a modern chaplain may be nothing like that, but the one thing they have in common with St

Peter is 'going to the place where the hurt is'. That must always be at the guiding principle for chaplains.

Throughout this book we will try to make sense of what chaplaincy is. Indeed who or what is a Chaplain? What makes them so?

I see quite a few people wandering around our port in high-vis jackets with "Chaplain" embossed on the back. Most of them I don't know: neither have I any idea of what their agenda might be. I suspect there is an element of proselytisation in what they are about and that is frowned upon by the port authorities and ship captains. Stella Maris does not support or encourage such activity in its Chaplains.

In my training capacity I emphasise over and over again, Chaplains are not merely a bunch of good people doing good things. Many folk do good things but does that make them Chaplains? I think not.

Our role as Chaplain is entirely rooted in service. Our vocation in ministry is a call to serve, following the example of Our Lord. This call to serve can take many forms though, in Stella Maris, it is made clear that ship visiting and hospitality are of paramount importance.

Liturgies on ships are not confined to Masses, for crews

will rarely have a priest available to them while in port. That is where our lay chaplains—and sometimes deacons —really make their mark. A chaplain may celebrate a Liturgy of the Word with a few crew gathered around. Likewise, if a lay chaplain is commissioned as an extraordinary minister in their parish, they may offer a service of Word and Holy Communion on board.

This is a very special way for someone called into this ministry to rejoice in their Baptismal sharing in the Priesthood of the Lord. The ongoing formation of chaplains must encourage them to be aware of Sacramental opportunities, should the crew desire such engagement, for isn't that in the very nature of chaplaincy?

As chaplains we engage not only with seafarers on ships or in centres but also with those in hospital, in prison, and in court. Our ministry leads us to stand alongside seafarers in times of trouble, wherever that may take us.

We have to be clear that we take out work beyond the realm of mere social action. Yes, there is a social element in our role, but that social action becomes sanctified in our conviction that the Lord walks with us on our daily journey. Among us there is such a conviction that the Lord graces the mundane, and allows us recognise the presence of our God in what would be an otherwise Godforsaken world.

We read in Matthew 7:9, *"Or who is there among you, who, if his son asks him for bread, will give him a stone?"*

The bread is a particular crisis or a heartfelt need expressed by a seafarer. The father is the chaplain, the one who gives, not a stone, but genuine help and moral support—the bread. Job done.

But then we might add "Have a piece of cake as well." That's chaplaincy.

15

BEING PRESENT.

The dreaded call from the Harbour Master came around midway on a bleak Immingham Sunday. I knew by the tone of his voice that this was not to be an invitation to a cosy lunch. "Colum, can you be on Quay Nine late this evening? There has been a major incident on a ship that left us two days ago."

The vessel in question was a small supply ship ferrying goods and services to the oil and gas rigs in the North Sea, so it runs regular and fairly short voyages. I was told the ship was returning prematurely, as three of the crew of twelve that had sailed from Immingham had died on board. No more information was given.

The rest of that day was mired in confusion. What would I find? How on earth would I deal with the grief of the crew? What would I say? What to say is often a worry for chaplain, for they are dealing with so many varied situations and cultures.

When I got to Quay Nine that night, other people were also waiting; police, accident investigators, agents. We stood around making polite conversation, but no one seemed to know what we would find when the ship berthed. The only new information I gleaned from the police was that the three bodies had been airlifted off the ship. They had been flown to the hospital mortuary, but there had been no mention of how they had died.

When we eventually boarded I went to the crew mess where a couple of the men knew me from a previous visit to the ship.

A lesson to chaplains: this is a time to be silent other than a casual greeting. I wanted to know how the crew had died, but this was not a time for questions. So I just sat, sharing the silence of the crew who mainly stared at the floor. There were tears.

Before I left the ship in the early hours, the Captain came to see me. Again he gave no explanation of what had happened, just a request that I accompany him to the mortuary to make a formal identification of his three crew.

We were driven there the next morning by the ship's agent. We made the journey in silence, other than a few words of admiration for the wonderful Humber Bridge. By that time I had been a priest for thirty-five years and had been called to the site of terrible road accidents and casualty wards many times. I wondered what horrors I might find in the morgue.

In the event, when the curtain was drawn back the three men lay on trollies. There was not a scratch on them.

The rest of that week was spent with the crew, some family of the deceased, the representatives of the shipping company, accident investigators—far too many people crammed onto a small vessel. There were many tears all round, and many unanswered questions. It did become clear that the deaths were the result of a tragic accident.

On the first morning at sea, the crew had complained that sleep had been difficult the previous night. There was a loud rattling noise coming from the base of the ship, and it was agreed this was caused by the anchor chain coming adrift.

Two men were given the task of securing the chain in the locker space. The first went into the confined space to secure the banging chain. The anchor chain locker was virtually airtight prior to it opening. It was estimated that the rusting of the bulkheads and anchor chain had, over time, used up the oxygen from the air in the chamber, leaving the air with about a quarter of the oxygen content needed for the men to stay alive. Consequently, once inside, the first man collapsed.

The second man raised the alarm and entered the chamber to help but he too collapsed immediately. A third man then tried to enter the small chamber wearing breathing apparatus, but could not get through the hatch. He tried again, using a different breathing apparatus, but when it became dislodged, he was exposed to the atmosphere in the locker, and immediately collapsed.

All three bodies were recovered by a team from the rig they were servicing. The men were airlifted to a local hospital where they were pronounced dead.

Of course there followed many investigations and the usual "Lessons will be learned," was trotted out many times. But the reality was that three men who had left their homes only a few days earlier were dead, and life for their grieving families would never be the same again.

We all know that ships and indeed ports can be dangerous places but the reality of that doesn't hit home until we are called upon to face the awfulness of it.

A port chaplain is always happy to respond to any need but sometimes we too feel overcome by the enormity of expectations put upon us. Again, what do you say, what do you do?

I find comfort in the wonderful words of Jesus to his disciples:

> *'But when you are handed over, do not worry about how to speak, or what to say; what you are to say will be given to you when the time comes.'*

MT 10:19

I carry those words with me and totally believe that the Lord will guide me in what to say—or more importantly, when to keep silent.

I cannot remember the details of what happened that week after the accident, except that I spent the time just being there, being present to the situation.

When helping chaplains understand their role, I lay great emphasis on simply being present. We have to acknowledge that we cannot change what has occurred, but we can be there to share in the grief, and people in turmoil appreciate that.

And what should we say to them? That is not an easy question to answer. God preserve us from the cliché. That's not what distressed folk need to hear; they've heard them a million times, maybe used the words themselves when confronted by the grief of someone standing before them. In Matthew's Gospel chapter 5 we see those salutary words '*Let your yes be yes and your no be no*'. Don't feel you always have to come up with the clever line or a perfect phrase.

This too, is when chaplains have to face up to their limitations, to know what we are, and what we are not. Pity the person who thinks they can do all by their own merit! Luckily we are not asked to.

St Paul, in his great wisdom said, '*There is nothing I cannot do in the One who strengthens me.*' Phil 4:13

God has created each of us to be uniquely gifted and talented. Nobody else can do what you do in the exact way that you do it. At any time in our lives, God may call us to focus on specific areas of ministry or giftedness, but He never asks that we do it alone.

16

UNUSUAL REQUESTS.

When a chaplain boards a newly arrived ship, he or she does so with a certain amount of excitement—but perhaps also a bit of trepidation. Will there be a friendly welcome? Invariably yes. Are there problems on board, maybe serious ones? Perhaps the basic question is 'Why am I doing this? On this horrible cold wet evening, why am I about to climb seventy steps into the unknown?' Therein lies the root of our chaplaincy.

We go onboard as part of the mission of the Church. We have been called in gospel terms to welcome the stranger and to be alongside those for whom life at that moment may be particularly challenging. The mandate for this is clearly laid out in the Gospel of Matthew 25:35-37.

It is a great privilege to serve the Church in this way, and shame on us if our ship visiting ever becomes tiresome or mundane. There is no place in sea chaplaincy for a short cut mentality that urges us to get on with it, to get it done.

Of course, every experience onboard is not going to be uplifting, but it would be good to judge a visit on the basis of the difference we have made to one or a group of seafarers.

It is no exaggeration to say that no two ship visits are ever the same. The ship may have been on a long voyage across oceans, or it may be on a short hop from a nearby European port. Whatever the length of the journey, the crew are likely to be tired.

A long time at sea will mean little chance of communication with family back home. When they come into port they are likely to request help with some sort of communication with the folks back home. And maybe it's been a couple of months since the last family conversation, and the news might not necessarily be good. Then the chaplain has a vital role to play in helping someone make sense of some tragic news from home.

This lack of communication can seem very strange to someone engaging with sea life for the first time; I'm thinking of new chaplains or volunteers. Maybe a bit of background information would help.

As I have said before, a seafarer is generally on contract for about nine months. That means working every day, usually six hours on, six off. The crew is generally pretty well looked after with regard to food and salary. About eighty per cent of their salary is paid into the family bank at home and the rest kept in the Master's safe as spending money when they arrive in port.

An emergency at home usually means a seafarer will search for a money transfer shop to send home their spending money to help with the unexpected bills. Although, as I said, crews are generally cared for, that is not always the case and we will look at some of those incidences in the pages ahead. The work is hard and mostly demands great skill. The sea can be a cruel and unpredictable workplace.

Just as every visit is different, so too are the many and varied requests we get from the crew. They can be simple requests, like asking for a SIM card or an internet connection, or maybe for a lift to the Seafarer Centre or a local shop. But occasionally the request may be on a more serious level; help with unpaid wages or lack of food. And then some have taken me completely by surprise and stay in my memory forever.

We had an Indian crewed ship with us for quite a long time because of the slow discharge of a delicate cargo. I had visited the ship a couple of times and enjoyed the company of the charming crew. One morning I spoke with the Captain and told him I had use of the bus that afternoon and offered to take the crew out for a few hours. I suggested a few possibilities, shopping mall, a visit to the beautiful city of Lincoln. He said he would ask the men their preference and let me know on my return.

Sixteen men filed into the bus that evening.

"Where would you like to go?" I asked.

The Captain replied. "We would like to go somewhere where we could walk on grass." A simple request—but understandable from a crew who had spent the last few months walking on the hard steel of the vessel. My eyes were opened to a harsh reality of the shipping world, things we merely take for granted.

So we went a local churchyard, the men took off their shoes and socks and for about an hour trod the long grasses and lawns. At one level this was a simple experience, yet on another, a profoundly spiritual hour when these men commuted with nature and experienced the joy of embracing God's creation.

Pope Francis was later to expound on this in his encyclical *Laudato Si*. At the conclusion he prayed

> 'All powerful God, you are present in the whole universe, and in the smallest of your creatures. You embrace with tenderness all that exists.'

They walked mostly in a silence they were unlikely to experience for the remainder of their voyage. You'd think I'd enabled them to have a glimpse of heaven, and maybe I did. I had, in a small way, made something possible for a group of men who would probably recall that beautiful afternoon as they crossed the oceans encased in vast structures of steel.

A few months later I got an email from the Captain with a picture of some of the men by the Church. He spoke of a very difficult voyage, and of some hostility from port authorities they encountered along the way. The pictures on their notice-board reminded the crew of the welcome and understanding they had received in Immingham, for which they would always be grateful.

This welcome and understanding is given by Stella Maris' chaplains around the world, and may God continue to bless their dedication to seafarers.

When training new chaplains, my mantra is clear: never underestimate the value of the small gesture. And that was another of those small gestures that can have such a profound and lasting effect on the recipient.

An unusual request came from Edward, a Polish engineer on a small feeder ship. He wanted me to take him to Toys'R'Us for he had heard they sold Thomas The Tank

Engine socks. His young son would be delighted to receive these when Edward next went home on leave.

Does that sound trivial and a bit of a waste of time? I don't think so. It only required a small effort on my part to allow a man separated from his young son for four months to do something that would bring great joy to his son—and of course, to him.

Another occasion that I remember with a smile was December 23rd, one of those filthy days we get around that time of year. It was only around 3pm, but already it was becoming dark. Heavily laden skies showered us with sleet in a biting wind.

"Shall we go back to Immingham?" I asked my companion.

"Let's do one more—we can bring Christmas greetings one more time."

The roads were quite slippery with the snow and sleet beginning to take hold.

When we got to the ship we found a team of eleven men sat around waiting for the evening tide that would take them out towards Finland. After a while the Captain received a message, which he read aloud. "The supplies ordered for Christmas can't get through. I'm sorry, everyone. It looks like our Christmas feast will be limited to the few tins left in the galley."

Gloom descended on the group.

"You've managed to get through," the Captain grumbled to us. "I'm not sure why the agent cried off."

"Why don't we take you to the supermarket?" I

suggested. "It's only a few miles away; we should be back in plenty of time to sail."

They took us up on the offer eagerly, and all squashed into the minibus. The massive store and massive carpark were both completely crammed. There seemed to be thousands of shoppers and trolleys inside. It was heaving; but about an hour later the crew emerged with trollies full of every imaginable wish list of seasonal food and drink.

We eventually loaded everything, and had just set off when a voice shrieked from the back seats, "Lemons for the Captain! We've forgotten lemons for the Captain!" So the process started all over again!

When we finally got back to the ship we helped them unload, and what joy a simple trip to the supermarket brought! I hope they enjoyed a very special dinner, and of course, the Captain his lemons...

Chaplaincy brings us into many places like that. A simple request often has a story behind it. Shame on us if we see these as trivia or a waste of our valuable time! Long periods at sea bring their own stresses in ways we can rarely imagine.

I was chatting with Bryony, a chaplain colleague, about unusual requests while on board ship.

"What's the strangest request you've ever had?" I asked her.

She smiled. "There was one time when when two young seafarers on a ship visiting Immingham asked if I would be able to help them.

"They wanted to buy suits for their weddings which were both happening later in the year. They were going to buy them online, but I wanted to make sure they had something that would be suitable for

such a special day. They were allowed a few hours' leave and I took them to get properly fitted and find suits they were happy with. They were like children in a sweet shop, running around to pick out suits and ties and try them on.

"After he got married, one of the guys sent me this picture of him and his wife on their wedding day, thanking me for my help."

These are the pictures the seafarer sent, and don't they look happy?

A small gesture such as this can make a huge difference, and one which the seafarers and their families will remember their whole lives.

17

A CAPTAIN'S DILEMMA

Skipper, Captain, Old Man, Master, Chief: I have come across these titles where the leader of the ship's crew define themselves. So too are these names (and more) often used by the crew themselves.

Under the law, the Captain is ultimately responsible for aspects of operation such as the safe navigation of the ship, its cleanliness and seaworthiness, safe handling of all cargo, management of all personnel, inventory of ship's cash and stores, and maintaining the ship's certificates and documentation.

They have to maintain a balance between the ship owners' demands and the needs of the crew. A good captain usually oversees a happy ship where the crew respond well to his or her instructions. I have been very fortunate to have met many fine Masters, who are often glad to have someone different on board with a different conversation.

The opposite can be true. I have met with a good number of unhappy ships, where the Captain has been held in pretty low esteem by his crew. There could be many reasons for this. He might be a shouty leader, barking out instructions, someone who cannot cope with the mixed races on board and is deemed to give preference to people of his own nationality. There could be any number of reasons. But let me tell you of a captain for whom I have great admiration.

I got a call from the Harbour Master (why do so many of my stories begin with that line?) to tell me, yet again, of a death onboard a ship that was just about to berth on Quay Eleven.

I boarded the container ship in the early hours to be met by a crew, mainly from Thailand, who were in great distress at the loss of a young deckhand. It was a silent welcome and a tearful one, for the death had occurred in the past hour, as the ship began its approach to Immingham. Police and accident investigators were already there and making their enquiries.

Since the ship had just arrived, the crew were busy at work, preparing for the containers to be offloaded. A container vessel is generally in port for a few hours; they get one load of containers off, and get the ones brought last time back onto the ship again. Even though a crew member had died, no time allowance was made for it in the schedule, so there was not much chance to talk with anybody who might want to do so. I stayed on the ship until coffee break came, when the crew came to sit with me, and told me the story.

Anyone who works with seafarers will know how often people are lost overboard, and it is always a tragedy. However, this one was particularly poignant.

As the ship had approached Immingham one of the crew thought it would save a bit of time if he started undoing the lashings on the containers. The shipman nearest him saw the danger and shouted at him to come out of that zone, but no matter how loud he shouted, he couldn't make himself heard over the roar of the engines.

One of the metal bars that kept a container locked in place must have been loosened. It sprung back suddenly and hit the lad on the head, sending him overboard. It was pitch dark, and nobody could see where he fell in the water.

Buoyancy supports were thrown in after him ,but remained untouched and it was clear that the body had been quickly swept away in the vicious Humber estuary tide. Life boats and nearby fishing vessels searched in vain for the body, and to this day it has not been recovered. Presumed dead, lost at sea, they said. Despite the regularity of this sort of accident, it was a terrible shock.

The men went back to work and as I was about to leave, the Captain came into the mess room and asked if he could have a chat.

He said, "Thanks for coming to the ship. We have many visitors tonight. The police and accident investigators have asked many questions, as you would expect. We are in bits—and yet the crew have to continue their work to get the ship turned around for an early morning departure."

Then he told me of the guilt he felt about what had happened, not that he could have done anything to save the man for he was far away on the bridge directing arrival procedures. What he was feeling guilty about was that he should have sacked the eighteen year old a month earlier.

"It was his first voyage and I quickly spotted he would never make a seafarer. He couldn't take orders or follow procedures. Last month he messed up big time by ignoring a fairly basic rule.

"I know I should have sacked him there and then—but I thought of the shame he would face back home if he was sent home early from his first voyage, so I decided to give him another chance. And now look where that chance has left him."

No words from me could lessen the guilt, so I just sat and listened to his outpouring.

As I left the ship, he smiled and said, "Thank you for coming to see us." Simple words but heartfelt, from a man suffering such grief. Some of the crew waved me off as I signed out, broken men but still gracious. I have often thought about that night but never came across the crew again. I suspect they were transferred to a different route.

If I had been in that Captain's shoes would I have made the same choice to give the boy a second chance? It's a real dilemma.

What would you have done?

18

CHAPLAIN AS PROPHET.

"God has created me to do Him some definite service. He has committed some work to me which He has not committed to another. I have my mission. I may never know it in this life, but I shall be told it in the next. I am a link in a chain, a bond of connection between persons.

FROM MEDITATIONS AND DEVOTIONS,
"MEDITATIONS ON CHRISTIAN DOCTRINE,"
"HOPE IN GOD—CREATOR", MARCH 7, 1848, ST.
JOHN HENRY NEWMAN

Vocation calls us to become the person God intends us to be. That is an ongoing journey through life; we never arrive. I am often saddened of hearing on Vocation Sunday "We pray that more will come forward to offer themselves for the priesthood and religious life". This limited understanding of vocation misses a great opportunity to empower the laity to celebrate their role as partakers in the ministry of the mission of the Church.

At Baptism we were all anointed as Priest Prophet and King, sharing intimately in the life of the risen Lord. The words may be frightening, or off-putting, and lead us to a 'not me' kind of response but the activity of the Church in the world would be more significant if that call was properly understood.

Stella Maris is a wonderful example of how this call, received in Baptism, can be used to drive the ministry of lay chaplains.

Other forms of lay chaplaincy have increased in the past twenty years or so. We have lay hospital chaplains, school chaplains, prison chaplains. It would be enriching to understand this, not as a result of diminishing numbers of  priests, but as an awakening of the understanding of a lay chaplaincy that brings its own giftedness into the realm of ministry.

> "Lay chaplains do not exist to help a busy priest, but to live out their anointing in Baptism as Priest, Prophet and King. But ministry can never be an individual response or personal choice. A person cannot undertake ministry on his or her own initiative. Ministry belongs to the church and not any individual". (Mullin. Study in Pastoral Theology. 2014)

We now have in place a formal commissioning process —the public ecclesial recognition of chaplaincy through local Bishops. By this the whole Church community, especially the local parish, recognise the special grace of ministry in their midst.

With these thoughts in mind, I would like to reflect on one of the calls of our Baptism: to be a prophet.

It is difficult enough to persuade chaplains of their gift-edness through Baptism; to get them to understand their call in terms of prophecy is a mighty task. But let's look at it.

In Isaiah chapter 6, we hear the voice of a reluctant prophet:

> *"Woe is me! I am lost, for I am a man of unclean lips and I live among a people of unclean lips."* (5)
>
> *One of the seraphs in attendance touched his lips with a coal for cleansing.*
>
> *Then I heard the voice of the Lord saying "Whom shall I send? Who will go for us?".*
>
> *And I said "Here I am, send me"* (8-9)

In the all the prophets we find reluctance, statements of inadequacies but also the voice of God reassuring the chosen one of his presence wherever they may go.

So, too, with Jeremiah we find the same reluctance but similar assurance from the Lord.

> *"Lord Yahweh, I do not know how to speak." Then Yahweh stretched out his hand, touched my mouth and said to me, "There! I have put my words into your mouth."* (Jer 1:6-9)

In Acts 2.17-18 Peter recalls the words of the Prophet Joel:

> *'In the last days I shall pour out my Spirit on all humanity. Your sons and daughters shall prophesy, your young people shall see visions, your old people dream dreams.'*

Prophecy is not about foretelling the future like some

sacerdotal fortune teller. The prophet speaks the Word of God to whoever will listen.

God seeks the care of the downtrodden, those least protected in society. God wills the end of oppressors who, from a lofty position, mock the afflicted and do them harm.

God wishes that all be set free, and their dignity respected. It is the duty of the prophet of whatever generation to do what they can to turn that vision into reality.

The Old Testament prophets were very much on the side of the oppressed, provided they were faithful to the calling of the Lord. They were people very much of the present, able to read the signs of the times, contemplate them, and analyse the consequences if matters didn't improve. They were honest and forthright with the people to whom they spoke, insisting that bad things would come the way of all who turned their backs on the loving God who called them and loved them as their own.

Prophets had a special mission to stamp out injustice when a people cried, seemingly in vain.

So how does this apply to chaplains?

The prophet knows the past promise of God's word, but knows how to interpret this word in her or his life and to speak that word to others that will lift them up. Every day we carry out that prophetic ministry.

I often say (you've probably gathered that by now!) "Never underestimate the small gesture, the smile, the word of welcome".

Those are prophetic acts, for we transmit through our words and actions something of the love of God to those with whom we share the moment. And in the bulk of our work, are we not people empowered by the call of the gospel and our Baptism to raise the lowly, the downtrodden, the people on the margins? That is the work of a prophet.

In the times when crew cry out to us about an injustice on their ship, we don't rush to conclusions, but 'read the signs of the times, contemplate them, and analyse the consequences if matters do or do not improve' before we act.

No one is saying it will be easy—the prophets of the Old Testament seemed forever to be anguished people. A prophet has to carry a heavy burden. It will be frightening when called to respond to injustice, and is never easy to confront those who create the injustice.

Will the situation improve, or will we make matters worse? A seafarer will often play down an injustice as if there is no other way. I think on the many times I have heard the phrase "Such is the life of a seafarer": but the prophet will be on the lookout for another way.

Today, in the midst of many situations of seeming hopelessness, it is easy for us to be overwhelmed and numbed. We feel unable to meet the challenge of delivering new life on behalf of those who feel hopeless and marginalised.

As in the Old Testament, a modern day prophet (chaplain) will say that it doesn't have to be this way. It is not easy to persuade a seafarer of this truth. There is a fear that to complain will make life very difficult in the present, and limit possible future contracts. Being blacklisted is a constant fear, for there are many people chasing a limited supply of jobs.

Those are the calls a prophet has to make through communication with the one '*who will put the words into your mouth*', in prayer.

For that's our role; we are priests and prophets. We are

to bring God's goodness, God's love, God's tenderness, and God's justice into our world, in our everyday life.

But just like the Old Testament prophets, we must be prepared for rejection and criticism. Jesus experienced plenty of this in his ministry—why should we expect anything less in ours?

But how do we keep going on days when the darkness of rejection weighs us down?

Our own faith and belief have to remain strong. We need to keep reminding ourselves that we are not alone, that the God who called us to look after the oppressed and the downtrodden will always be with us, for it is his work we are doing.

> *"Before I formed you in the womb I knew you. Before you came to birth I consecrated you, I appointed you as prophet to the nations."*
>
> (Jer 1:5)

19

A PROBLEM BEFORE MASS.

They said it was to be the biggest ship ever to visit Immingham. There was great excitement in the port and the local press ran an article describing this as a great coup for Immingham. It was also to be the maiden voyage of the ship which was to bring cargo from Singapore, have a turnaround of one day and make the return voyage. The full crew, including the Captain, was Filipino.

On the morning of the planned sailing, I received a call from the berthing company asking for my help. Half the crew had walked off the ship and the remainder had locked themselves in the engine room. It is extremely rare for a crew to take matters into their own hands like this.

I met with the crew in an office compound, and the full horror of their plight unfolded.

Conditions for the crew were so bad that they wrote a letter of complaint to the company, whose representative visited the ship on arrival at Immingham. His response was to threaten them with the police and assure them they would all end up in prison: obviously an idle threat, but the crew were at the end of their tether and refused to work.

Their letter of complaint highlighted the following issues:

- No pay in the two and a half months they had worked for the company.
- No receipt of danger money they were promised for double watch shifts while sailing through the Gulf of Aden.
- Lack of food on board; they had survived on a diet of boiled rice, twice a day, all the way from Singapore, a voyage of nineteen days.
- No bottled drinking water or fruit juices on board.
- No access to shore leave in Immingham. The Captain told them it wouldn't be possible. (He didn't want them to have the chance to complain).
- No communication with families.

The staff at the berthing agency was wonderful and provided the crew with sandwiches and bottled water. They were very sympathetic to the plight of the crew but really needed to get the ship away to allow for new arrivals that were booked on the jetty.

I went on the ship and met the owners' representative and told him that I was happy to negotiate with the crew, but there could be no more idle threats and the concerns of the crew had to be addressed: they refused to come back on board while the Captain was still there.

By this time we were joined by the ship agents who had travelled up from the South, and calls were made to the company offices in Japan.

The realisation had begun to set in that there was a serious problem with the current Captain who had neither shown care for the crew, nor presented the shipping company in a good light.

A long day of negotiation ended with the promise that the Captain would be replaced and would spend a night in a local hotel before flying home. The crew were taken to the centre where they were able to make contact with their families and there was a mixture of relief and yet some fear that their complaints would come back to haunt them.

Next day I arranged for a representative of the ITF (the International Transport workers' Federation) to come on board and he was able to deal with the wages issue. A Fleet Manager arrived from Japan and I was invited to join in the discussions he had with the crew.

A new captain would arrive at midnight, the ship was to receive a full quota of provisions, as listed by the chief cook; wages would be paid on time and various technical issues with the ship would be properly addressed.

The cook was a happy man when I presented him with a bundle of blank pages and asked him to write his wish list.

"Hold nothing back, your wildest dreams!" I told him.

He sat with some of the crew and compiled a list that would have done the Ritz proud. Yes the basics were there, the water, bread and rice but so too the steaks, chickens, sides of pork and lamb, a shoal of fish and shellfish, beer, various and copious quantities of soft drinks and cordials.

When I went back and handed it to the agent, he stared at the paper. "This is outrageous! The company will never agree to it!"

"Fine," I said, "but the ship goes nowhere till all this is delivered."

It came the next day.

What is difficult to understand is that it was costing the company up to twenty thousand pounds a day to keep that ship on berth.

What sort of mentality inspires a company to pay that rather than feed and pay the crew?

All that remained was to celebrate Mass and bless the ship. That was a very joyful occasion. Prayers were said for their families and the joy with which they received Holy Communion made me realise what 'hunger for Eucharist' really means.

Again, this highlights the plight of some modern seafarers, unable to have their voice heard, even when the nature of their complaint is so apparent.

So maybe find a moment in your prayers to remember those whose rights can mean so little in this cruel world of the sea.

20

PAUSE FOR THOUGHT

Sometimes, in the most unlikely of places, you may hear something that make you see things in a new light. I was on a plane. Awaiting takeoff, a part of the safety briefing really caught my attention, though I must have heard it hundreds of times before.

"In the unlikely loss of cabin pressure, an oxygen mask will drop down in front of you. If you are travelling with a child or someone who needs assistance, secure your own mask first, and THEN ASSIST THE OTHER PERSON."

When we are caring for others—the weary, the sick, the broken-hearted—we have to make sure that we ourselves are in a fit state; we must put our safety masks on first so that we can help others. If you are in this position (and I suspect many of us are) make yourself breathe in a bit of space, make yourself breathe in a bit of free time. If we don't, we won't be able to support others in their needs.

So the next time you are on a plane, pay attention to the flight attendant. You never know, it might just save your life.

21

THOUGHTS ON CORONAVIRUS

When I started writing this book in 2019, life was quite normal. However, as we go to press in the summer of 2020, we're living in a very different world.

Coronavirus has spread across the globe. Four million cases have already been diagnosed and here in the UK, we have been in lockdown for nearly two months.

Thousands are dying, our churches are closed, people's movements are limited, and the world cries out for normality, or even an explanation of what is happening.

We are not used to being taken by surprise, and we don't like that. We are not in charge; we have lost our control—perhaps it's a time to be humble, to cast aside that arrogance. It is so easy to see God at work in the happy times of our lives and we thank and praise him for that, but now?

Maybe you recall the words in John's Gospel of Martha after the death of Lazarus. *"Lord, if you had been here this would not have happened."*

But the Lord is here.

"Yes, I will be with you to the end of time." These are the

final words in Matthew's Gospel: yet in these previously unimaginable days, that presence may be hard to grasp.

Let me take you back fifty years to my days in seminary.

Our Theology Professor, trying to explain the presence of God, was reading aloud that same passage from Matthew's Gospel. Then he brought the bible closer to his face and continued to read, but with greater difficulty. Finally he held the text tight against his face where he could no longer read and said, "That's how close God is, so that we cannot see Him."

Never forget that presence.

I hear it often said that we are all in this together, in the same boat, but I look at it slightly differently. We are sailing through the same storm—but not in the same boat. We are all on different ships during this storm, experiencing a very different journey. We are all just fighting our way through the storm.

On land, many are in isolation in their homes or places of care, uncertain of what the future might bring. There is worry about jobs, food deliveries, wages, the welfare of loved ones—and even life itself. Our churches are closed and we are missing the presence of the Lord in Holy Communion.

Seafarers understand all about these things; they have been a part of their lives for as long as they have been sailing. For seafarers, they often come together in the space of one voyage.

They worry about wages—will they be paid this month? Will the chandlers get food to the ship in time? Are family safe at home? Are their jobs safe for another contract?

We can learn so much from them about coping in these times we call unfamiliar, times that cause us to be so fearful. For them, lockdown begins on every voyage once the gangway is raised, hatches and doors fastened. Irrespective of the size of the crew, the long hours, even months of isolation must be a drain on mind and soul.

On land we still have our creature comforts, things which are luxuries to those at sea: hot showers, more space, a non-rocking kitchen. Most of us are still able to go for a walk outside. The food shops keep us supplied despite the selfishness of greedy people who see no further than their own needs.

We long for normality, to stop living in isolation from one another, but we may have to wait some time and the normality we seek may never return. Unfamiliar times indeed.

They are unfamiliar in a different way for the seafarer, used to coming into port to be greeted by a Stella Maris chaplain who does everything possible to make their lives a little better, things great and small.

That welcome is now on hold because of the safety

needs of both chaplain and seafarer, but we hope and pray that normality may be resumed as quickly as possible. However, another welcome comes to them now in virtual form through social media and is as heartfelt as ever.

Though we cannot visit the ships for now, we are still very much connected in our prayer and care for each other. And how very necessary that is in these present times of great uncertainty!

This year even the Easter services have been cancelled, and for the Church, Holy Week is the most significant religious week of the year. In a busy few days from Palm Sunday to Easter Day, the Church pulls out all the stops to heighten the significance of the death and resurrection of Jesus. Liturgical planning groups meet, choirs practice, readers practically know their texts by heart and nothing is safe from the rub of the Brasso cloth.

This year our churches were empty, choirs were silent and the great story of our salvation was to put on hold. The rota for those volunteering to have their feet washed remained unsigned, yet again. Palms may be stored for next year, and maybe the music too, but still we lose so much. The loss is great, but we know that it is the right thing to do in these strange times.

Seafarers rarely have a chance to proclaim Easter while on board, and yet when I have celebrated Easter Mass with them, I have been overjoyed to find such faith and under-standing of the place of service in Easter. Not for them any reticence about volunteering to have their feet washed—everyone on the ships asked for it.

At sea, seafarers have come to understand that although Holy Communion may be a rare occurrence on ship, the presence of God is ever real and a constant support; so close that we cannot see him.

Perhaps this is something else we can learn from them —our understanding of the Lord's presence has been too dependent on churches being open and masses being celebrated. Maybe the absence of our liturgies will help us to better appreciate the significance of the Easter celebration when we can sing "Alleluia!" with our friends once more.

As for me, the reality of being in isolation really hit me hard on Holy Thursday.

For forty-six years I have celebrated the ceremonies of that day, my favourite celebration in the Church's year— the procession to the stillness at the altar of repose, gentle moments reflecting on the horrors to come for Jesus and, even more significantly the unique feature of that day: the washing of feet, as Jesus did for reluctant disciples at their final meal together, a profound example of what the call to service means. None of this was possible this year, in what I call 'COVID times'.

On Holy Thursday, we celebrate the washing of the feet as an example of the call to service. This is echoed at present as the importance of washing our hands is stressed, a simple act but one so relevant and important to now.

That got me thinking.

Hands.

Not only the washing of hands, but hands serving and supporting in this time of world crisis—the serving hands of 'key workers'—a list of so many. But then, what about the serving hands of family in such acts as washing, preparing food, holding, soothing; the fingers that tap texts, messages, phone numbers, emails and video applications to stay in touch with loved ones at a time when we are all so separated.

The hands of Jesus feature prominently in the Gospel stories. Gentle hands that healed not just those who maybe thought themselves worthy, but hands that touched lepers, the outcasts and untouchables of their day. He was not afraid to touch others, as we are just now with our distancing rules.

Hands that held the broken hearted, fed the hungry and gave sight to the blind. Wounded hands that healed so many in body and mind—and were then nailed to a cross.

Our serving hands are needed now more than ever to send the same message of love, humility and acceptance. Are they open? Generous towards a needy person, those depending on our provision, cooking a meal for the lonely, elderly, writing a note to a friend needing encouragement, palms held together in prayer…

Our hands can do His work every day and become a blessing to others. There is more significance to our hand-washing than just soap and water: let it be a cleansing of hands ready to receive from others and, cleansed of self-ishness, to be offered in service of others.

On Holy Thursday we also think of Jesus in the Garden of Gethsemane. For Jesus this was a time of waiting in great anguish and loneliness, for even his disciples had fallen asleep. He was alone in the garden, absorbed in prayer to the Father.

This is our Gethsemane, aware of the great suffering around us and waiting to find meaning in all of it. More suffering lies ahead: our Good Friday has yet to come before we dare anticipate Resurrection. May that Divine presence be a source of strength and comfort in these dark days.

The Lord is near to the broken-hearted, He helps those whose spirit is crushed. (Psalm 34)

~

During these COVID times, many are beginning to feel the loneliness and lack of human comfort and are broken-hearted to hear of the death of so many. Such contemplations led me to think about someone I have ignored for too much in past years, my Guardian Angel.

Dear Mrs McKenzie, my very first teacher, would begin our school day with the prayer:

"Angel of God, my guardian dear,
    to whom God's love commits me here,
    ever this day be at my side,
    to light and guard, to rule and guide."

As children there was total faith in our angel but somehow maybe we got a bit blasé and pooh-poohed the idea of needing an angel to guide our ways. We became confident and sure in our own strength and ability, and closed our minds and hearts to the idea of needing a spiritual friend. But maybe the lesson of these intensely isolated times is that we need our angels more than ever.

Our tradition has always taught that from our birth a Guardian Angel is given to us to guide and protect us, to accompany us with every step; the angel of every breath we take. This is not some abstract spirit, but someone who is as close to you as your skin.

Why not reacquaint yourself with yours, maybe even give them a name?

In this time of great anxiety I find it such a comfort that in Scripture, where angels usually bring a message from

God, the first words of that message are often "Do not be afraid."

One of the saddest things I hear with this disease is that people are dying alone, not allowed the consolation of loved ones. But they are not, as this is where I see the final act of our Guardian Angel; to be with us when nobody else can, to whisper gently "Do not be afraid," and lead us back to where we first met for this voyage.

There at our first breath, and our last.

In my lockdown I cannot leave my house at all, which means I only see the images of what's going on in the outside world. One remarkable picture is people locked into boxes, two metres away from each other—the queueing outside supermarkets.

I've never had to do that, and I tried imagining myself in that situation. I would be nervous in my little square with an eye on those around me, watching to see if they dare sneak an inch into my space. I'd be anchored to the spot until I got called forward into the next square.

Pondering on this led me to something far more familiar to me—ships queuing at anchor, waiting on their turn to come forward into the next slot until they are eventually called into the great marketplace of the port.

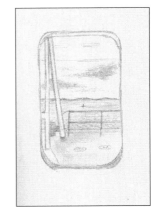

Being shut away with my own anchors I live in hope, not some vague aspiration that things can only get better.

Beyond my window I see signs of spring all around. The beauty of buds, shoots and blossoms all whisper that new life is coming. I see the extraordinary selflessness of people helping the less able. I rejoice at the skills of those who can save lives. The world around me is blooming, signs of promised hope bursting forth in a rich abundance.

God asks us to be still, to treasure that richness while remaining anchored in his love. In due course, on the fine tide that faith tells us will come, we can raise our anchors and store them safely aboard. We have this hope as an anchor for the soul, firm and secure. It enters the inner sanctuary behind the curtain. (Hebrews: 6.19)

So join me in hope. Be still, attentive, let your heart be open and astonished by the immense love that God has for all of us.

We are anchored in love and hope; though the storm is dark, it will come to an end in time, and we will find ourselves in calmer waters again.

Let us sit together, at least in spirit, and watch for the new dawn.

22

AT SEA, AWAITING ORDERS.

AT SEA, AWAITING ORDERS.

I like that phrase. It describes the status of a ship unsure of where its next cargo is to be found. When cargo is discharged, the Master may not know the vessel's next destination, but staying tied up in port awaiting a call would be a very expensive option. So immediately after discharge a vessel will transfer to anchor, awaiting the call from the Company.

If a ship is on a regular contract, for example, carrying biomass from Canada, the Captain may well sail slowly in that general direction, confident that the next orders will direct him there.

At Sea, Awaiting Orders: it sums up how we spend a lot of our time, not just as seafarers but in many aspects of life. In times of worry or doubt, or when faced with a problem way beyond our capabilities, we wait for guidance. We wait for someone we trust to steer us in the right direction. And of course the right direction might not always be to our liking but if we trust someone, and if that someone is the voice of God guiding us in prayer then we are more likely to take notice.

Stella Maris supports all seafarers, irrespective of nationality or denomination, in the harsh and cruel maritime world. Whatever the nature of that help, be it spiritual or material, it will be given freely with open and generous hearts.

Pope Francis in his book 'The Name Of God Is Mercy' writes

> "It is necessary to go out: to go out from the churches and the parishes, to go outside and look for people where they live, where they suffer, and where they hope." - Random House 2016

He invites us to tend to the wounds of those on the margins and that this is the essence of the mission of Stella Maris.

Awaiting Orders.

This year we celebrate the centenary of this great mission and we wonder where we go from here. The world and needs of the seafarer have changed out of all recognition in that time. It would be naïve to think that we merely carry on as we are doing, but I am confident that whatever comes our way, Stella Maris will respond to that world, bringing the love of God to where people are hurting.

For one hundred years, through the work of chaplains and volunteers from all walks of life, Stella Maris has been the key provider of welfare to the people of the sea. This welfare has taken many forms to enhance the spiritual and temporal wellbeing of those to whom it has been called to serve.

You have just read about some of those encounters, and I hope the experiences of a chaplain in one UK port gives some insight into the vast amount of Gospel-inspired love that has been central to this extraordinary charity. Multiply that by several hundredfold and you will sense the enormity of the work of Stella Maris throughout every continent.

And what of the days ahead—will the charity be replicating this work for another hundred years? Recently, I spoke with Martin Foley, CEO of Stella Maris UK and European co-ordinator, and we pondered what the future might hold for us. It is right to celebrate a centenary of great achievement, but how foolish it would be to wallow in that success without an eye on the future.

Martin said, "The shipping industry is continually changing and adapting to meet the needs of the commercial world, so that it can become more competitive and cost-effective. Improvements in ship technology, structure and materials will lead to even bigger vessels, particularly within the container shipping industry.

"So too there is a greater awareness of environmental issues. There is constant pressure to reduce the carbon footprint of the world's shipping fleets, and this will only increase into the future. These issues will impact on the lives of seafarers. Perhaps crews will become smaller with a new emphasis on skills to adapt to new technologies.

"So much is uncertain. The needs of those at sea are changing all the time, and developments in the maritime industry will determine many of those needs." He continued, "What we can say with certainty is that wherever there is a seafarer in need, Stella Maris will be there to give a welcome, a hand of friendship and a prayer of blessing."

When I started out in this work sixteen years ago, I was astonished at what was expected of seafarers; long contracts entailing many months' absence from families, long hours of work, often monotonous, little free time to share with other crew who may not share culture or language, difficulty of communication with family, and many other things.

Fortunately, the communication technology has developed. Gone are the days of taking seafarers to phone boxes in remote places, changing money to have enough coins for the call, and then perhaps finding the phone out of order. Can you imagine the frustration of that? All they could do was go back to the ship to sail to a new country and find different coins to try the process all over again.

You may remember being on holidays abroad in the days before mobile phones, waiting in long queues with a pocketful of loose change, to chat with someone you may see in a few days, anyway. No such luxury for shipping crews.

Now every seafarer has a mobile phone, a lifeline to be charged and topped up so that when in an area where there is enough signal, the voice of a loved one can bring great joy and consolation. The things we take for granted!

But where next? The world of communication technology is changing at pace, hopefully making life more normal for the crews around the world. Communications may improve, working hours may lessen, good food on ships may be taken for granted and wages paid on time.

But as Martin pointed out, irrespective of the changes in the world of shipping, what will never change is the commitment of Stella Maris to be a beacon of light, a ray of hope for dispirited seafarers. That will never change because the principles of the charity are based on the command of the Gospel that we go to all nations to proclaim a message of love to those on the margins, to the downtrodden.

At the beginning of his public ministry, Jesus lays out the direction of that mission by quoting from the Prophet Isaiah.

"The spirit of the Lord is on me, for he has anointed me to bring the good news to the afflicted." Luke 4:18

His final instruction before ascension indicates the road we must follow.

"Go therefore, make disciples of all the nations...and look, I am with you always; yes to the end of time." Matt. 28:19,20.

So our calling will not be one limited to a small group where we may feel comfortable, but to all the nations.

Stella Maris proclaims that mission to the entire seafaring world, ever confident that the Lord will be with us as we fulfil it. But who will carry out this great commission of scripture in the future?

Martin and I reminisced about the great characters who have served as chaplains or volunteer ship visitors over the years. And there have been many. Men, women, lay, ordained, who have touched the lives of distressed crew, whether lonely souls who are 'lost' at sea, injured men hospitalised in a foreign country while their ship has sailed, folk trying to cope with the death of a crew member on board or news of a family death thousands of miles away... These are just some of the tasks carried out by our colleagues over the years.

It is right that we remember and celebrate this great

work, but many of these good people are no longer around, and we have to plan for a future without them.

Martin spoke of the importance of recognising the work of the laity; in fact, the original Apostolatus Maris began as a lay organisation. Fortunately, today there is a greater understanding of the role of the laity in the life of the church, no longer mere passive participants, but sharers in the mission of the church.

In the mix of charisms, ordained and lay, that has driven the work of our apostolate over the years, there has been a recognition of shared but differentiated responsibility for that mission: working together on equal terms, seeing our different vocations and gifts as complementary and mutually enriching.

In the years ahead there is a likelihood we will have fewer priests, so that particular charism may be lessened. Greater reason, therefore, to promote the value of the laity in all we do. This is not some wishy-washy notion but is based on the reality of the priesthood of the baptised.

I remember many years ago as a young curate we welcomed Bishop Gray as auxiliary Bishop of Liverpool. At his first mass with us he said that up till then he thought the greatest day of his life was the day of his ordination to priesthood but this surpassed that for now this was the greatest day of his life, called to share in "the fullness of Christ's priesthood."

A few days later when Archbishop Beck introduced him to the full assembly of clergy he mentioned that remark and commented "I think he left out THE most important day of his life. When journalists asked St John Paul II, shortly after being raised to the papacy. if this was the most important day in his life, he said, 'No. That was the day I was baptised.'"

The wide-ranging topic of the priesthood of the

baptised needs a much fuller investigation than is relevant to these pages, but Stella Maris in its formation programme is keen to enable its chaplains to understand their baptism as a springboard to all they do in ministry.

Stella Maris engages the services of coordinators in key places around the world, Australia, Asia, North America. I asked Martin about his role as European coordinator.

"A common factor in our roles is the development of Stella Maris within our various regions. We give support to areas that are strong and self supporting. Likewise we offer services to areas where perhaps Stella Maris is in the early stages of growth. At the moment Denmark is an area where our help and experience is being used to work alongside the people there to help them build on the good work and energy of the Stella Maris community.

"I'm not saying that in the UK we run the perfect model, but I'm aware of the strength of what we have achieved here, and our duty to share that expertise when asked for help."

We look to the future with great hope, because our call to mission is in response to the Gospel command to walk alongside the stranger among us. Pope Francis constantly refers to us as disciples and urges us to go to the margins in search of those who have no voice.

May we always be the voice of the downtrodden,
be alert to the cry of the needy,
listen attentively to the call of the Lord,
and position ourselves
...At Sea, Awaiting Orders.

ACKNOWLEDGMENTS

Thanks are due to our proofreaders Rosie, Hannah, Will and Angela who have pored over theses pages and been of enormous support in the final production of the book.

A special thanks to Bryony who has graced the pages with her imaginative and inspiring sketches, and the wonderfully evocative picture we have used for the cover.

A very special thanks to my dear friend Josie Edwards whose skill and enthusiasm put this book together. She inspired and cajoled in equal measure. Her only instruction to me was "Give me text, give me more text!" She took some musings of mine amassed from sixteen years working in Immingham port, ordered and I think beautifully arranged them.

I hope you found them interesting and encourage you to support the wonderful charity that is Stella Maris.

Fr. Colum Kelly

ABOUT THE AUTHOR

FATHER COLUM KELLY has served Stella Maris for sixteen years and is a priest of the Diocese of Leeds which he served in parishes in West Yorkshire.

A keen football fan, he has been a spectator at some of the most horrific incidents of recent years. He was present at Heysel, Rome, Hillsborough and though not at the Bradford Stadium fire was called into the hospital to support the bereaved and injured.

He loves music, poetry and most sport, but finds nothing more exhilarating than taking to the road on his Honda Pan European.

∾

JOSIE EDWARDS was ten when Colum arrived at her home parish, and she spent the next six years watching the church become a really cohesive community, full of laughter and love, packed to the rafters even on normal Sundays.

She has been involved in independent publishing for some years as author and editor, having set up her own small press. She was delighted to help when Colum finally agreed to commit words to print, and is really proud to have been involved with this book.

She lives in Hampshire with her lovely husband and mischievous dog, has blue hair and laughs a lot.

TO FIND OUT MORE...

Fishermen's Mission:
  https://www.fishermensmission.org.uk

Markfield Institute of Higher Education
  www.mihe.ac.uk

Mission to Seafarers:
  www.missiontoseafarers.org

Sailor's Society:
  www.sailors-society.org

Stella Maris:
  www.stellamaris.org.uk

Facebook:
  https://www.facebook.com/StellaMarisOrg/

Twitter:
  @StellaMarisOrg

BIBLIOGRAPHY

New Jerusalem Bible, Darton, Longman & Todd, 1990

Bergoglio, Jorge / Pope Francis, tr. Oonagh Stransky: The Name of God is Mercy, Bluebird, 23 Mar 2017

Julian of Norwich - Revelations of Divine Love, OUP Oxford, 2013

Mullin, Study in Pastoral Theology. 2014

Newman, St John Henry: Meditations and Devotions, "Meditations on Christian Doctrine," "Hope in God— Creator", March 7, 1848

Wicks, Robert: Perspective: The Calm Within the Storm, OUP USA , 27 Mar. 2014

Printed in Great Britain
by Amazon

85574251R00071